M000222806

Fatherless Son

Rashod Coleman

thank you for your support

Author Rashod
11-15-2020

Copyright © 2020 Rashod Coleman
All rights reserved
No part of this book may be reproduced without the author's expressed permission.

PROLOGUE

A LIFE WORTH LIVING

4:00 AM

I wake up before the alarm goes off to stretch before my workout. I turn off the alarm before it goes off so that I don't wake my wife.

Ten years ago, Amy and I met at a coffee shop called Vigilantes. I can still picture her with those red bottom heels, a gray pencil skirt, a black V-neck shirt, and a million-dollar smile. I've always been open to dating women of different races, so it was no surprise to my mother and father when I brought a white woman home.

Amy continues to sleep. I remove our $5,000 sheep-fabric blanket from my body. The blanket was shipped in from Egypt two weeks ago from a street merchant my wife met while doing humanitarian work. It was a gift recommended by my father, who runs our real estate company from the United States.

As I sit up on the side of the bed, I smell eggs cooking in the kitchen. Our family maid, Mellisa from El Salvador, works the early shift. She lives in the sleeping quarters one hundred feet from our house in a small cottage I employed Amish builders to design. Since I was a child, I have always loved my eggs scrambled, over easy. Mellisa makes them to perfection.

I kiss my wife and walk out the door to head to the gym for a quick ab workout. I exercise four days a week, supplemented by one family jog on Sundays after work.

Today is Friday. So Tony, my personal trainer, likes to do a really tough ab workout right before the weekend. Amy, who cooks healthy meals every night, usually doesn't travel with me on the weekends, making it hard for me to maintain a healthy diet. Tony likes to inquire about what I ate over the weekend when I return home Sunday night, and for that reason, we try to get ahead of the curve by knocking out the ab work first thing Friday morning.

As I walk into my 2,000-square-foot gym, Tony hands me a green smoothie, and we start walking on the treadmill. On an average day, we'd do a full-circle walk around the compound, roughly 2,000 acres of Africa's best forest and Greenland — but not today. We walk for about 10 minutes on the treadmill, then hit the ab workout.

Tony and I finish, and I walk into the shower, where I have a water-proof television broadcasting CNN. The Palestinian Army, Hezballah, has just sent rockets over the Israeli border; and Israel is now planning how they want to retaliate. I scream out to Raymond, my assistant on standby, "I need to head to Palestine!"

"I'm on it, sir," he replies as he walks out of the room, dialing numbers on his cell phone. Raymond has worked with me for about six years now.

I met Raymond at an NAACP fundraiser I attended six years ago at Howard University in Washington, DC. At the time, he was working for the catering company hired for the event.

As he stood by our table waiting on us, I sparked up a conversation with this 6'5" sophomore studying communication. During our chat, Raymond explained that his mother had moved to America from Uganda when he was just 12 years old. Raymond told a good story.

A great communicator and fluent in Arabic, Raymond made the perfect assistant.

Now, when I give him a task, it is already done 90% of the time. We often travel to the Middle East together. The food is amazing, and during our trips, Raymond serves as my English-Arabic interpreter. Raymond, a devout Muslim — me, a practicing Christian — makes us an awesome team. I've been working with the leaders of Palestine and Israel for years, and we are so close to a 2-state solution I can taste it.

Why would the Palestinians be so reckless during such a sensitive time for both countries? I need to get there, and ***quickly,*** *before President Larnoff makes an emotional decision.*

I leave the shower and put on a suit designed by Steve Harvey. The outfit consists of gray pants, a matching blazer, a polka dot shirt, and a white tie. Before I head to the vehicle that's on standby, I run up to say goodbye to my children: Luell, Rashod, and Esmé.

Luell, my firstborn, studies the Central American banking system and Spanish. She's only 9 and already so far ahead of the game. Her favorite food is an El Salvadoran dish called pupusas.

Rashod Jr. is six years old. He studies Mandarin (and speaks it) with a focus in Asian politics. The boy loves sports, and Kobe Bryant is his favorite player.

At three years old, Esmé is our youngest. She speaks Arabic and a little Hebrew. She will study religion in years to come.

While they sleep, I give each of my children a kiss on the cheek. I walk out of my front door and jump into a black Escalade. We drive to the other side of the compound, where a helicopter awaits us. Raymond hands me the phone with President Larnoff of Israel on the other end.

I greet President Larnoff in his mother's native tongue: "Shalom, Mr. President."

"Good morning, Rashod."

Regarding his response to Palestine, I ask President Larnoff not to make a decision before I talk to him face to face. He responds, "Only if you bring some of Amy's cookies."

Typical of President Larnoff. We're on the brink of WWIII, and he's joking.

I look to Raymond. "Did you bring any?" Before I finish, Raymond opens a black lunch box with Amy's cookies inside. "Mr. President, it's a deal." I can feel him smile through the phone, cocking his head to invite me over. "See you soon." Raymond and I climb into the helicopter, and it lifts off.

As we rise, the helicopter turns west toward Israel. Taking in the view below, I reflect on where I am in life right now: Three beautiful kids who speak different languages and have traveled the world. A wife that does humanitarian work across the globe and manages to make it home for dinner every night. I, a Harvard graduate with a Bachelor of Arts in Foreign Affairs.

I started off my public service career in the state department. Since then, I've grown my small dream of solving world conflicts into a multibillion-dollar consulting firm that brings world leaders together to pursue a more peaceful world.

For example, last year, we raised 150 million dollars at a dinner that ended in a down-to-the-wire chess game between President Mohamed of Palestine and President Larnoff of Israel. President Mohamed won, though President Larnoff accused him of practicing on the side with a world champion to show him up that day. It was all fun and games, of course.

The two had been strategically placed next to each other at the dinner, surrounded by a room full of fellow world leaders. I knew President Mohamed likes hot sauce on his fish, so my coordinator intentionally placed the hot sauce in front of President Larnoff. For President Mohamed to get the hot sauce, he would have to first speak to President Larnoff. This broke the ice to what I thought was a great night of fun competition.

This is the life I was supposed to live. Full of joy, entertainment, excitement, travel, and history. My destiny. Instead, in the early morning hours of February 21, 1987, The Newark Police Department of Delaware snatched it all away. Taken from me before I could even try to obtain the dream God had set out for me.

CHAPTER 1

A HURT LIKE NO OTHER

In June 1982, my mother, Linda Coleman, became pregnant. At that time in her life, she was a tall, slim, dark-skinned, hardworking 20-year-old woman with a three- and four-year-old son. She was reluctant to have any more children because she had dreams of going back to school and finishing her college education. She was raised in a household of women. Being the middle child of three girls, she was forced to grow up quickly. Her father died when she was just four years old from cancer. Her mother worked long and tireless hours for a wealthy Asian family out in the suburbs. During that time, most African American women without educations were forced to work as maids for rich families who wanted help around the house. Like many African American children at that time, my mother and her sisters were forced to fend for themselves.

Because Linda was always the tallest person in her class, she would often be the target of bullies and their jokes. Unbeknownst to them, she was known to be a fighter.

A friend of hers once told me, "Your mom fought the whole school one day. They were picking on her, and she was just swinging at all of them." That same spirit of fighting would come in handy later in life, but it wouldn't be at school. It would be at people sworn to protect her.

My father, Daniel, had a rough upbringing. Shortly after being born in Newport News, Virginia, to a Mr. and Mrs. Coleman, Daniel and his family migrated to Chester, Pennsylvania. They would eventually settle down in Wilmington, Delaware. Daniel's mother went to church every Sunday, and like most devout African American families, they would attend throughout the week. As a school-aged boy, he often sneaked out of church on 22nd and Pine to play with friends. The church had many doors in the basement he would use to make his exit. After playing, they would return by the end of service in hopes of not being noticed.

In Daniel's youth, he would grow to have a strained relationship with his father. Being one of eight children, he would always find himself in trouble. Daniel's father would send him South at the age of 15 to live with his grandmother in Virginia. A couple weeks later, after Daniel refused to attend school, he was sent back to his father's house in Wilmington, Delaware. On the day of his arrival, Daniel's father ordered him to clean the basement. Daniel grudgingly walked down to the basement and exited out of the cellardoor to hang out with friends.

Hours later, Daniel returned home only to see his belongings in a black plastic bag on the porch. His mother met him at the door and explained that he was no longer welcome in the house. His mother then drove him a couple blocks away to a rooming home across town. After she briefly spoke to the owner, she paid the man a security deposit and first month's rent to allow her 15-year-old son to stay in his house. Cold and alone, Daniel would sit on his bed and cry as he gazed out of the window at the sight of his mother's vehicle pulling out of the parking spot. Life was looking pretty rough for my father, but soon things would begin to turn around.

My father and mother would meet on a bus the following year in 1975. My mother, Linda, was only 13 years of age but often looked after her siblings. With Linda's mother working long hours, they would often have the house to themselves. My father was a frequent guest at the home not only because he wanted to be around Linda but also because there was a refrigerator full of food.

At the age of 15, my mother had my oldest brother Levar, then Maurice, the following year. My father had always longed for a girl, but my mother felt the opportunity had passed. With some convincing from my father, my mother agreed to try for a girl one last time. On March 6,

1983, as everyone waited so patiently to see the sex of my mother's final child, an 8 lb., 13 oz. boy was brought into the world — to much disappointment. Although they wanted a girl, on that day, they promised to love me just as much as the other two boys. The doctor passed me to my mother and said, “This is the strongest baby I have ever delivered. Congratulations!”

My older brothers, Levar and Maurice, didn’t want another sibling. To get them on board, my mother had them give me a nickname. They chose “Doodles.” When asked why they chose that name, they simply said because it sounds funny. If that wasn't bad enough, my father already had a female’s name picked out. Cameal. Do you want to even take a guess what my middle name is? You got it. Cameal. Historically, this was a great day for our family. They passed me around like a doll baby checking out all of my features. Things were perfect for our family of five, but this would soon take a turn for the worse.

Three years later, on February 21, 1987, my mother got a collect call from Gander Hill Prison. The voice on the other end was my father, Daniel. He explained that while on his way to work, a police officer stopped him about a crime that recently took place in the area. He said, "They released me after questioning because the victim said, 'I don't think that's him.' Hours later, the police showed up to my job and placed me under arrest, claiming to have a photo of the victim and me."

After an intense interrogation in which my father claimed to be repeatedly called nigger with guns pointed in his face and threats to be hung, the police contended that Daniel admitted to the crimes.

Five months later, the 22-year-old white woman who initially said it wasn't my father took the stand and made the argument it was him. The case was further pushed by Delaware's top white prosecutor, though the trial presided in a black judge's courtroom. The prosecutor was known throughout the state to be fierce during questioning, especially when it came to putting black, uneducated men behind bars. He was the top rape prosecutor from 1980-2003. The jury consisted of 11 Whites, one Black.

At the end of a two-day trial with the whole courtroom sitting on the edge of their seats, the judge told the defendant to rise so the jury could announce their conclusion. "We the jury of the state find defendant, Daniel Coleman, guilty of two counts of first-degree kidnapping, first-degree robbery, and third-degree sexual assault." At this point, my mother could only wish that the black judge would show some leniency for my father — wishful thinking on her part.

On October 15, 1987, when I was only four years old, the judge and jury would forever alter my family's path. After banging his gavel three times to quiet the crowd in the courtroom, the judge looked at my father and said, "Double life plus five years!"

My shocked mother had to be helped out of the courtroom by friends who showed up to support her. Like a well that's run dry, she had no tears to cry. She wanted to but couldn't. The past five months, she'd cried while reading the news, thinking about the father of her children spending the rest of his life behind bars. Tearlessly, Linda held both hands over her chest while looking at the ceiling, seated, her heart thumping a million beats per second. The shock was so great, she froze and couldn't get out of her seat. She slouched and buried her head between her legs.

When she returned home to my two brothers and me, we had no clue what happened to our father. As I played in the living room with my favorite toy, a trash truck, could she ever fathom I would grow up to become a part of the same system that caused our family so much pain? Being the person who I am today, it's hard to grasp the reality that the State of Delaware labeled my father a Sexual Predator. Was it true?

CHAPTER 2

FIRST TIME

In the following months after my father's sentencing, my mother decided to move us out of her mother's house. She found an apartment on the west side of Wilmington to give our family a new start. Her fears of one day being a single mother were inevitable at this point. Though she felt that the cards dealt her were unfair, there was nothing she could do. Her sleepless nights of shedding tears would eventually come to an end, not because she wanted them to, but because they had to. These three little boys needed their mother and father; therefore, Linda was forced to play both roles.

The home my mother found for us was a two-bedroom apartment in a community called Canby Park. The neighborhood was locally known as "Hidden Valley" because it was tucked away at the bottom of a steep hill. The community consisted of roughly 20 three-level buildings. In each building, there were 12 apartments with four apartments on each level.

Our apartment was on the third floor, the first door on the left-hand side. Walking into our apartment, you would see a living room on the left, followed by the kitchen, and lastly, the kid's bedroom in the back. On the right was the dining room, followed by the bathroom and my mother's room, facing the kid's room.

My mother, at the age of 23, was now on her own. With no financial help from her husband or the government, she obtained a safe environment for us to live in. Even though times were rough, my mother always kept a smile on her face.

One Sunday morning, my mother packed us in a car and told us we were going to see our dad. The idea seemed pretty cool to me, but as a four-year-old, I thought it was weird he wasn't living with us. The ride was long, but for the most part, I played in the backseat with my toy wrestlers and dumpster trucks.

We eventually pulled up to this massive complex with a weird looking wired fence around it. It was a regular fence, although it had a circle of barbed wire around the top of it.

After my mother parked, we got out of the vehicle, and she said, "Make sure you take everything out of your pockets."

I stood there with my Hulk Hogan action figure in my right hand, mesmerized at this huge building until my mother said, "Rashod, you can't take toys in there. Leave it in the car."

"Why not?" I replied with a voice of confusion.

"It's considered a weapon, and they won't let you in," she answered sternly.

Crushed, I reluctantly put the toy in the backseat as tears began to build up in my eyes.

She fixed our shirts, tucked them in our pants, and brushed our hair before we went in.

In the lobby, my mom had my brothers and I sit next to each other on these blue plastic seats. There were probably twenty to thirty other children there with their parents. As each family walked in, they seated their children and got in line to talk to the man sitting behind a glass window wearing a blue uniform with a shiny badge on his shirt. When my mother was finished speaking to the man in uniform, she walked back to us and handed all three of us a plastic badge with a metal clip. I couldn't get my badge on, so my oldest brother, Levar, clipped it to my shirt.

Throughout our time sitting in the waiting area, these older gentlemen, around forty-years-old, wore bright white one-piece suits cleaning up the waiting room. I couldn't help but notice they all had DOC written on the back of their clothing. They had a look on their faces that was neither happy nor sad. They seemed to just be present in the moment, not necessarily tuned in to what was going on around them.

While I pondered where in the hell I was, a man walked in with a uniform and badge to make an announcement. I didn't listen, but at the conclusion of his speech, my mother directed us to get up and stand in line.

"Where are we going now, mom?"

"We have to go through the metal detector," she said, annoyed.

After every two families went through the metal detector, there was a loud noise that startled me for a second. It was the sound an alarm makes when it goes off in the morning. After the sound stopped, a rusted, blue steel door would open, and the families who just walked through the detector would enter. They didn't go far because I could still see them through a skinny, rectangular window on the steel door. After enough people entered the small space on the other side of the door, that same door electronically slammed shut behind them, which would startle me again.

In front of us was a family with a newborn baby. The baby couldn't have been more than four months old. Mother carried the baby through the detector, which didn't make a noise, signaling there was no metal. However, the guard told the woman to place the baby on the table. He proceeded to search the baby for something.

My mother looked in astonishment and said, “My God” while shaking her head. I would learn later in life why the guard performed that act on this infant, but at the time, it didn’t seem necessary.

Our time had come to walk through the doors. Nervously, we went through the detector, and it didn't go off. By this time, I was used to this alarm-like noise, so it didn't startle me when it went off to allow my family to walk in the door. As the door closed behind us, I felt a chill go through my body. Mentally, I was shocked that I was in a place I couldn't exit. At this point, we were locked in.

The alarm went off again. We moved forward into another section. We were outside, but there were those weird fences in front of us and on both sides. We waited there until the other families were screened and let into the same section. After everyone was in the same 15' by 20' section, the electric fence opened, and they herded us into the next passageway like a bunch of sheep. We reached a door to go inside, but the door behind us wasn't secured, so the door in front of us wouldn't open.

I had so many random questions and thoughts at that point. *Who are all these people I'm walking with? Is everyone here to see my dad? Is he leaving with us after this?* I was also wondering what my Hulk Hogan action figure was doing in my back seat.

While waiting for the door to open, I could faintly hear people yelling from the windows. I couldn't make out what they were saying because the windows were only cracked. Although I could tell they were screaming as loud as possible.

The door finally opened, and we all were gathered into an open room with about 30 steel tables. Each table had four chairs around it. My mom picked one of the tables while my brothers and I sat down. She remained standing.

The alarm sounded off for the doors to unlock, and everyone's attention turned towards a specific doorway. Out came about 25 men dressed in white jumpsuits, like the men in the waiting room. At first, they seemed to walk in a straight line, then broke off to their respective tables as they located their visitors.

As much as I tried to reach for a picture of my father in my head, I couldn't.

Was he tall, short, fat, skinny, light skin, dark skin? I just didn't have a clue. Later in life, I would read his court testimony, which would clarify why I didn't know what he looked like exactly.

After about 11 men — mostly African American — walked into the room, there was this tall, light-skinned man walking towards our table.

I contemplated in my head, "Is this my dad?"

To my surprise, it was him!

He embraced my mother with a strong, long hug. She wrapped her arms around him and turned her head to the left as she placed her head on his shoulder.

He whispered in her ear, "I love you, Linda. I love my family."

My mother began quietly weeping as my brothers, and I sat on the chairs watching this heartfelt moment. It was the first time I saw my mother show that much emotion. She was always so tough and strong, yet at the moment, she had a protector.

"Y'all are going to be alright," he said. "We are going to get through it. It's all lies."

I had no clue what he was referring to, but I could tell something bad had happened. When I got in trouble, my mother always sent me to my room. Maybe Dad got in trouble, and they sent him to this big place with loud noises and weird fences.

After about a minute, they released each other and turned their attention toward us.

“Get up and give your dad a hug,” my mother said with a smile, tears in her eyes.

Levar hugged him first, followed by Maurice.

Then it was my turn. Daniel put his arms around me and picked me up in the air. As I hugged him back, there came a sense of awkwardness over me. I realized at that point that this was my first time hugging a man. He was muscular and had facial hair that scratched my face as he pulled me close to him, and I realized I had never experienced male affection before. It was foreign. The only people I ever gave hugs to were my mother, aunts, and grandmother.

Eventually, we all sat down, and my father picked me up to sit on his lap.

He smiled and said, "How you doing?"

"Good," I said.

Mom and dad talked to each other for the most part, but every now and then, he would break off and speak to us.

After some time, I asked my dad what he eats in this place.

"Ummm, we had fish, potatoes, and vegetables last night."

“That sounds good,” I replied.

"Nah, it's horrible," he said, smiling.

As they continued to talk, my attention was directed to a gentleman walking around the room with a camera. He stopped by each table and spoke with the person at the table that everyone was there to see. After speaking with them, the entire family walked over to this makeshift background and took a polaroid picture. He gave the photo to the families and went on to the next table.

When he approached our table, my father gave him a nod and then told my mother, my brothers and I to go over to the makeshift background to take a picture. As we posed, a sense of comfort came over me. A sense of being protected. Anxiety I didn't know existed exited my body. For once, my mother didn't have the burden of making everything happen for us, and that felt good inside.

After taking the picture, the man gave it to us and walked off. I looked up at dad and asked, "How much do you pay for the picture?"

"Ummm, I'll give him stuff," he replied.

"How much money?"

"We don't have money in here, son. I give him smokes."

Because my mother didn't smoke or drink (at least not in front of us), I had no idea what smokes were, so I continued to press.

“Smokes? What are smokes?” I said.

He looked at my mom, and she said, "Cigarettes."

“OK,” I replied.

About 20 minutes later, a guard began walking around, giving a signal to each table. My father saw the guard coming and told us all it was time to go. He gave all of us bear hugs and said he loved us. I wanted to ask him to come with us; nevertheless, even as a four-year-old, I knew that wasn't possible. He and my mother engaged in a long, passionate kiss before our departure. Because my father was so light-skinned, you could see he had red lipstick all over his mouth at the end of their kiss. My mom spent the last 10 seconds with him trying to wipe the lipstick off of his face. He continued to look back as he walked to the same door that he came out of. There he was. My father.

The one who birthed me. But can't come home with me.

CHAPTER 3

MAMA BEAR

A year after moving into the apartment, my mother introduced us to her new boyfriend, Roger. Roger moved into our apartment not long after meeting my brother and me. He was the first man I can remember living with, so there was a sense of protection that he brought to our family. He was a tall guy, at least 6', brown skin tone and muscular build. Roger was a pretty quiet guy who kept his hair cut and dressed nicely. He rarely came out of my mom's room to interact with us, but he always had a smile on his face when he did. During the times my mother was at work, he mainly kept his distance, so my brothers and I basically had the apartment to ourselves.

On a Saturday morning, around 11:00 AM, my brothers and I sat in our living room, eating cereal while watching cartoons. My mother was working, and Roger was in her bedroom, playing music. As our eyes were fixed on the television, suddenly, we heard the front door handle turn. We all looked back at the door with concern because we knew our mother wasn't getting off work early. We could still hear the music from Roger's room, so we knew he was still in there. A wall to the left of the door blocked our view from immediately seeing who walked in. Suddenly, a white or Hispanic man with thick reading glasses, dark hair, and a tan jacket came walking in. We froze. He stood staring at us. I thought for sure this guy was going to kidnap, sexually assault, or even kill us. He didn't say a word. He just stood there, motionless at the entryway. After a couple of seconds (which felt like an eternity), we all started screaming: "ROGERRRRR, ROGERRRRR, ROGERRRRR," at the top of our lungs. When the intruder heard us screaming, his body twitched, and his eyes opened wide as if he had just snapped out of a daze. With no explanation, he turned, walked out and shut the door behind him.

About 10 seconds later, Roger came running from the back room with no shirt or shoes on.

"Some guy just walked into the door," Maurice said.

"Who was he? What did he look like?" Roger replied.

After we told him, Roger stormed out to look for the man. Roger came back about five minutes later and said he didn't see anyone.

Hours later, our mother returned home. My brother and I told her what happened. She was shocked! She gave us all a big family hug and said, "I'm glad everyone is OK, but let's remember to keep the doors locked at all times."

I never said anything, but I was the one who accidentally left the door unlocked. I knew mom wanted to be there for us more than she was, but who else would pay the bills?

At the time, she worked a full-time job at Delaware Charter and a part-time hostess gig at Perkins Restaurant, so her time at home was limited.

Two days later, my mother and I walked to a shopping center located next to the Canby Park apartments. We needed more breakfast food for the following weekend. As we walked around a corner, standing right in front of us was a face I would never forget. I pulled my mother's coat jacket and whispered, "There he is, mom. There he is!"

"Who?" She said, with a puzzled look on her face.

"The guy that walked into our apartment the other day. He has the same coat and glasses on."

Frightened, I began walking backward to get some distance away from the man, but my mother had other plans.

She grabbed my shirt and said, "Are you sure?"

"Yes. Let's go, mom." I feared he'd recognize me.

"Stay right here and don't move," she said as she began walking towards the man.

"Excuse me, sir. My son said you walked into my apartment the other day?"

The man glanced at me with a puzzled look and said, "Ummm..."

She quickly cut him off with a tongue lashing while standing in a boxer stance with her right finger pointing into his face.

"*Ummm,* nothing, motherfucker! You touch my door handle again and watch what happens to your ass!"

The puzzled look on his face quickly turned to sorrow. He walked the opposite way with his head down and without uttering a word.

My mother walked back to grab my hand and said, "What kind of cereal do you want? Frosted Flakes or Fruity Pebbles?"

"Fruity Pebbles," I said with a smile while squeezing her hand with satisfaction!

That was just my mom. She was like a modern-day Superwoman without the cape. Never backing down from anything or anyone. In that situation, the message was to face your problems head-on. Unfortunately, soon, we would be forced to run.

Months later, in the middle of the night, I woke up to the sound of screaming from my mother's room. My brothers Levar and Maurice, were already awake plotting something.

Maurice said, "We should go in there and help mom."

Levar responded, "Man! Look how small we are; we should go call the police."

I was now six years old, Maurice ten, Levar eleven, so Levar's rationale made the most sense.

My mother was in the room, arguing with Roger. About what, we didn't know. Roger was on crutches because of an injury he sustained while playing basketball. When he came home with the crutches, I tried to walk with them, but they were too tall. He told me not to play with them because they were bad luck, and I might end up really needing them.

As the screaming intensified, I heard my mother scream, "NOOOOO," followed by a big boom that shook the apartment. Next came a forceful glass shattering. My mother burst into our room and ushered us out of the apartment.

"What was that noise?" Maurice asked as my mother grabbed

her pocketbook and slammed the front door behind her.

"Roger and I got into an argument, and he tried to throw the television out of the closed window," she replied.

With no car and wearing our pajamas, we ran to my aunt Brenda's house, which was only about a half a mile away. By this time, it was roughly two o'clock in the morning. My aunt Brenda had three kids and a two-bedroom apartment; we knew we couldn't stay there long.

Mom banged on Brenda's door and yelled her name three times. Aunt Brenda always went to sleep around 6:00 PM, so the chances of waking her up at two in the morning were slim. Fortunately, we saw a light come on in the apartment window, and someone moved the curtain to look out.

Moments later, Brenda came to the door in her pajamas and said, "What's going on?" Confusion on her face.

My mother said simply, "We need to stay here for the night." She ushered us into Brenda's house, putting her hand on the top of our heads, while we walked by her and Brenda.

"Girl, he tried to throw the television out the window. It broke the glass but didn't go through," my mother said.

Aunt Brenda made us all makeshift beds in her living room, and I slept pretty well that night as my mom and aunt stayed up talking.

The next morning, I woke up to knocking at my aunt Brenda's door. Roger. Mom just sat on my aunt's recliner chair, shaking her head. Maybe we were supposed to be scared at that moment, but we weren't. I went to the window to see who was out there, and I saw Roger in the yard screaming, "Linda, I'm … I'm sorry, Linda."

He was still on crutches. Hopping around in the yard, crying.

He spotted me at the window and said,

"Doodles, tell your mom to come to the door."

My mom told me to sit down on the couch and be quiet.

He left after about 30 minutes.

Eventually, we would go back to our apartment, and sometime after Roger moved out. I saw Roger on a bus about 20 years later, and all I could think about was that incident. It took everything in me not to punch that dude in his mouth. Before he got off the bus, he attempted to shake my hand, but as my mother did prior, I didn't budge. He was dead to me!

CHAPTER 4

MAN IN THE HOODIE

Summertime. Heading into the third grade, our family moved to 104 North Franklin Street in Wilmington. It was a large four-bedroom house — lovely compared to our apartment at Canby Park. Franklin Street was only about a mile from Canby Park, but it was a whole new world. As a seven-year-old, I was amazed at the noises of the mostly African American and Puerto Rican neighborhood. Police sirens, fire sirens, vehicles blasting loud music, and couples arguing were the norm. I had to adjust quickly if I wanted to survive.

The 100 block of Franklin Street had rows of homes on both sides of the street, with one-way traffic that could fit two vehicles. Our house was two doors down from a bar called Safari Lounge. Though Wilmington residents attended it during all hours of the day, it was mainly a nightspot. On days where I would sleep in my mother's room — a regular occurrence — I knew when they were shutting down because everyone frequently stood out front of the lounge, including our steps through all hours of the night. If the crowd lingered too long after closing hours, they were often dispersed by Wilmington Police telling patients they had to, "Keep it moving," officers yelled as I tried to sleep.

On a Sunday afternoon, while walking to a store located on Lancaster Avenue and Harrison street corner, my focus was on these two African American males on the corner of Reed Street and S.

Franklin, which I could see while walking to the store. As soon as I turned left to head down Lancaster, my mother yelled, "Doodles?!"

I made a U-turn, walked past the Safari Lounge, and made a right back onto Franklin street, where she was leaning halfway out of the door.

"Yes, mom?"

"Get a quart of milk when you're at the store."

"OK, mom."

I made another U-turn, then made the left turn back down Lancaster Ave. I saw the guys from earlier still standing on the corner, conversing with each other. Another man walking in their direction, who they couldn't see because they were facing my direction, was walking with sort of a limp from their rear. The male wore blue jeans, a blue jean jacket, and a black hoodie underneath. My attention stayed on him because, as he walked up, he kept looking back as if someone were chasing him. With both hands inside his front pouch, he looked behind him one last time and tightened his hood. Finally, the two men looked back at the man with the hoodie. The two males took off in a sprint running down Reed Street, a cross street to Lancaster Ave. About five feet away, the male in the hoodie pulled a black metal object out of his pouch.

POP POP, POP POP!

POP POP, POP POP!

That was probably the loudest sound I had ever heard. So I watched the situation transpire like slow motion.

Before the loud POP sounds, I could see a spark coming from the gun. As the two guys scrambled not to get hit by gunfire, one of them grabbed his own leg and continued hurriedly limping down the street. Before I knew it, the guy with the gun was gone.

I ran back to my house and busted through the front door. Time sped back up. I yelled for my mom, who inquired about what had happened. I could barely gather my breath to tell her.

"Some guy was shooting. Over by the liquor store!"

"Who?"

"Some guy with blue jeans, a black hoodie, and…"

Her eyes glanced towards the door, still open. Several people outside noticed and listened to me. We heard police sirens grow louder and louder as officers arrived at the shooting location. Trying to gather my breath so I could tell the rest of the story, my mother slammed the door. "I don't want someone to throw a firebomb in this house."

She never took me to talk to the police station to tell them what I had seen. How could she? After what the police did to our family several years earlier, why would she trust the same people that gave my father a life sentence? We never spoke about that moment again. For the next week, I was afraid to even sit on the step, fearing that the guy with the gun knew I saw what he looked like. And if I were to go to the police station and give a statement, who would protect my family from retaliation? There was no man in the house, so my mother only did what she had to do to keep us safe. Usually, the man is the protector in the house, but when he is absent, women are forced into that position. No one on the streets ever approached us about that situation, so I guess, as a family, we made the right decision to keep our mouths shut.

CHAPTER 5

WELCOME TO THE WEST SIDE

Due to our move, all of us kids switched schools. I attended Shortlidge Elementary School, which was located on the north side of town. Franklin Street was on the west side of town; so, I was forced to share the same classrooms as students from the other side of town. I didn't understand the dynamic of being from one side of town or the other. During the prior year, everyone I went to school with lived in Canby Park, so we didn't need to pick a defined group of people to be friends with based on where we lived.

To say I was nervous on my first day of school is an understatement. My mother, who had landed a new job, rode the city bus to school with me the first day. As we walked into our new environment, I began to think…

What if I had my dad drop me off? A big strong man dropping me off would intimidate all these new kids.

As soon as I entered the first class, everyone stared at me, which didn't help my anxiety. I would later learn that I didn't have matching socks on, which is why everyone laughed at me. The teacher introduced me, and I took a seat in the rear of the class. I couldn't help but notice there were a lot of cute girls there. In particular, there was a girl named Tyra, who had a nice body and Chinese-shaped eyes. As we went to the lunchroom, I tried to walk behind her in line, but one of the other kids cut me off.

I'll talk to her later.

At the end of the day, I got on the school bus assigned to me and sat towards the middle. Everyone sat with their friends, so I was forced to sit by myself because I didn't know anyone. One of my classmates, Lenny, got on the bus last because he had gotten into trouble during class. Once he was on the bus, he smacked a kid in the back of the head. The kid didn't even look back at Lenny. I could tell the kid was scared to say anything to him because he kept looking straight ahead, both arms wrapped around his dinosaur trapper keeper. Not sure why, but it pissed me off that Lenny would do something like that. Halfway through the ride home, Lenny walked by my seat and gave the kid sitting in front of me a two-finger push on the side of the head. As I thought about standing up for this kid, I had to weigh my options. I could tell by Lenny's talk that he was related to the kids in the back of the bus. As Lenny walked back towards his other relatives, I said, "Yo?"

"What?" said Lenny with a smirk.

"Why don't you pick on someone your own size?"

"Like you?"

"Yeah, motherfucker, like me," I said, sharply.

Lenny shrugged. "OK, we'll fight when we get off the bus."

He continued to the back of the bus and told the rest of his cousins about our exchange.

Shit!

The kid sitting in front me looked back at me with the look of, "You must not know who he is...?!"

He was right, but I was no dummy. I looked back. It was about seven of them staring back at me.

We finally got to our bus stop, and it was time to get off. When we rode past my house, my brothers were sitting on the front step. With some quick thinking, I rolled the window down real fast and said, "Yo, I'll be there in a minute. I know mom is waiting on me."

My brothers didn't understand what I told them, so they just said, "Aight!"

I got off the bus and ran faster than you can imagine to my house. I ran home so quickly, my feet felt like they were burning. I wasn't about to get banked by them on my first day. I could fight, but I wasn't dumb enough to fight seven of them.

In the following months, Lenny would become my first friend. I found out later that Lenny didn't have his father in his life either. He was a lot shorter than me, but he had a huge family and everyone on West Side respected them. He would teach me a lot about being in a violent, drug-infested neighborhood. He taught me where not to walk at night, what "stick up kids" were, and who not to mess with in the community. There was a street a couple of blocks down from us named Reed Street that he told me to stay away from.

"Stick up kids are young guys who will rob you for your money, so try not to walk places by yourself at night. That dude right there caught a body before, so if he asks you to do something for him, make up an excuse as to why you can't do it," he said. Crazy that a third-grader was teaching me this, right? Those same lessons would ultimately save my life from ruin.

I realized that after being around him, he was one of the nicest guys in the world. When we were out of school, we had to dodge bullies. Conversely, when we were in school, Lenny felt like he needed to be the bully to gain his confidence back and not get bullied. As we got older, he turned his bullying tactics onto other bullies instead, and I thought that fit him well.

I sat with him at lunch, and he introduced me to Terrance, Casime, Fat David, and Bone. The five of us were all from the West Side, so we began to hang together. Terrance, who we called Doc, was born to be a comedian. My earliest memory of him was at the lunch table. We would all take turns making beats by banging our knuckles on the lunch table and rapping to it. Doc was the best at it; thus, he would try to take up all the time. One day, I jumped in and cut him off to make a beat and rap. He looked at me with a look of disgust and said, "Yo, you're ugly. You look like a piece of shit!"

I felt like the whole cafeteria laughed at me. I laughed along with everyone because Doc had said it in a joking manner.

Doc was this little dark-skinned kid with a gap between his top, middle teeth. Doc always had something funny to say and loved to make jokes out of any situation. He loved to dress nice and talk to the girls. When girls came around, rest assured, there was a joke coming your way. His nervous tic was to joke himself out of uncomfortable situations, and everyone knew it. His crazy personality would soon make us all feel like superstars.

Casime was a quiet kid — but sort of a bully also. His little brother, Fat Dave (who was in the same grade), would follow Casime's bullying tactics. I would come to learn that their dad was in prison, like my father. One day, Casime said his dad was sent away for drugs or something like that. He would always tell a story of finding a black trash bag filled with money. The brothers were two peas in a pod. If you got into a fight with one of them, you had to fight the other. It was unfair, but hey, it was what it was at the time.

Bone was the tallest out of us. Tall, brown-skinned, with a peanut head like the rest of us. Bone was a quiet dude that had the loudest laugh you could imagine. The time Doc called me a piece of shit at the lunch table, I can still hear Bone falling on the ground from laughter. Bone had a big brother in my brother's grade known around town for being really good at basketball. This made up our crew. There would be people that would add to our group, but this was the core of it in the third grade.

At the end of our third-grade year, there was buzz about a talent show. None of us had ever been in a talent show, and we were not sure if we had talent or not, but we wanted to be in it. The cost was $1 to enter the talent show, so we went to a grocery store to help people carry bags to cover our expenses. There was a new song out by a rap group called The Geto Boys. While traveling home on the school bus, we would rap their Halloween song every day. After much consideration, we decided to rap that song during the talent show.

The night before the talent show, everyone had to stay after school to allow the staff to see your talent. There were a bunch of kids there performing everything from ballerina to juggling. We performed the song in front of the staff, and they made sure all of the curse words were bleeped out. While practicing the song on our own, Doc would imitate the lead rapper of Geto Boys, who went by the stage name of Bushwick Bill and was a little person. We could barely finish the practices because Doc's imitation was so funny. On the day of the rehearsal, Doc said that he was not going to perform it until the talent show because he wanted everyone to see it for the first time. We all didn't understand, but we went along with it.

The following day, every kid in the school was packed into the gym. As we sat backstage, we peeked through the curtains and saw all of our fellow students sitting in the crowd. The number of people just grew bigger and bigger as each act performed. Finally, they gave us the signal that it was our turn. They started the song, and we ran out on the stage, rapping as if our lives depended on it. Doc stayed off to the side when we went out so no one could see him. We got through the first two verses, and the momentum started to die down. Then came Bushwick Bill's verse. Doc came from behind the curtains bent down, with his hands in his shirt, as if his hands were short, and he had his shoulders up, hiding his neck, contorting his body as if his body were the size of a little person rapping the song. He waited to make his entrance and rapped a couple of words before coming out so the crowd couldn't see him first. When the crowd saw him, there was a roar of laughter like I had never heard before. At the end of his verse, there was a standing ovation by the students and faculty. As they called the second and third place winners, we waited with great anticipation. Then the principal said, "And first place…the Geto Boys!"

We ran up to the stage and jumped around like we had just won the Super Bowl. Doc grabbed the certificate as everyone cheered for us. All of us stood up there, wishing we had fathers to see this moment. Despite that, we had a sense of accomplishment. It felt *sooooo* good. We had put our minds together and won the competition. We were stars, and no one could take this from us. We raced home to Third and Broom Street, where we played after school every day. Doc stood in the middle of the street with the certificate as vehicles drove by. It was such an amazing moment for us kids without fathers.

***

Years later, one sunny, summer day, Doc sat in a car with some friends on the same block we went to after winning the talent show. He was in the driver seat with a male friend in the passenger seat and a female friend in the back.

According to Doc's friends, a death angel walked by the vehicle that only Doc could see. He asked them who the man wearing the strange clothing was. The other two laughed because they could see no man walking around them.

All of a sudden, through the rear-view mirror, Doc and the others saw a black male, 5'7", in dark clothing, walking up to the vehicle. As the individual advanced, Doc reached in his pockets to get the keys out. But he fumbled the keys and looked up at the mirror. The male was no longer there.

POP POP, POP POP!

POP POP, POP POP!

The sound of a .45 magnum handgun.

As the shots stopped, the friend in the passenger seat saw holes in Doc's chest, followed by blood gushing from his torso.

"Doc! Doc! Doc!!"

No answer.

As the gunman ran off, Doc's friend recited a Muslim Prayer to Allah: "If it be your will, please receive my brother's soul."

The sound of police sirens became louder and louder as they got close. Police dragged Doc out of the vehicle and began CPR.

No use. The death angel would not go to God empty-handed that day. On May 7, 2016, Terrance Kinard was gunned down by an unknown male at 3:00 PM on the West Side corner. The very corner we so desperately loved!

CHAPTER 6

A WAY OUT

While walking home one night from hanging with Casime, I saw a flyer on a street pole: "Little League Football Tryouts June, 16 @ 4:00 PM". I ripped it from the pole and took it home to my mother. She looked at it.

"That's this Saturday."

"I know. Can I go?"

"Sure — just remind me."

At school the next day, I told Casime about the tryouts with a team called the Wilmington Redskins. My hope was that he would go to tryouts with me to see if we could both make the team. Neither of us had played organized football, but we both thought we were good enough to make the team. Also, neither of us knew this would be the start of a great friendship between the two of us.

We walked to the tryouts, which were located at Bayard Middle School. As everyone was talking, a tall, heavyset, brown-skinned man blew a whistle, and all the kids crowded around him. He started speaking with a loud, raspy voice that commanded attention.

"My name is Coach George. I'm the head coach of this team, and this is my assistant, Coach Roc. We have a lot of people out here today, and to be honest, there is no way that we will be able to keep everyone. If you are not picked at the end of this three-day tryout, don't be discouraged. That just means you have to get better at something, then come back and try again next year. OK! We are going to split everyone up in positions. I want you to go to the position that you think you can play. We will let everyone try out at that position, but if we need you somewhere else, you must be willing to be a team player and do what we ask. OK — when I blow the whistle, you need to move with a purpose." He blew the whistle.

As we all began moving, he blew the whistle again.

"Everybody stop and go back to where you just were. Hey, son, what's your name?

He spoke to a heavyset kid with an oversized white T-shirt, black basketball shorts, and unlaced cleats.

"Brandon," the kid said, confused.

"Hey Brandon, do you know what it means to move with a purpose?"

"Run, I guess!"

"Well, son..."

Coach called everyone "son," even though we were not his sons.

"What you were doing when I blew the whistle earlier was running, but it wasn't running with a purpose. There's a difference, son. Everything we do here is with a purpose. Let me show you."

There was a football shield about 10 feet away from where Coach George was standing. Every one of us young teens was staring to see what was going to happen next. Coach turned his hat backward and tucked his shirt in. Then, he put his whistle inside his shirt. He looked over at Coach Roc and said, "Give me one," which meant he wanted the whistle blown. When Coach Roc blew the whistle, Coach George ran as fast as possible over to the football shield, and all the players were laughing at how quickly and seriously he did it.

"That's how you move with a purpose, dammit!"

The whistle blew for all of us, and I ran as fast as I could to the wide receiver line. I chose this position because of my mother's current boyfriend, Kenneth, who loved the 49ers wide receiver, Jerry Rice. Kenneth would start screaming and yelling in the house every time Jerry Rice caught a pass. Looking back at it, I understand that it was the attention of a father figure and his approval that I was striving to get. But back then, to have a man around was simply something of a different feeling.

Once I got to the receiver line, I looked around for Casime and spotted him with the quarterbacks. The receivers and I started off by running 15-yard sprints to see who was the fastest. I was in the front, coming in first or second place on every run. Coach George and Coach Roc watched over the drills and jotted notes on a spiral notebook as the volunteers instructed us on what to do.

There were parents, mostly mothers — but a couple of fathers — watching their children try out. My mother had to work that day, so I knew she wouldn't be there to see me.

We all lined up side by side with one orange cone on both ends of us.

“Set...go!” the volunteer screamed as we all ran to the next cone.

I could hear coach George’s voice in the background as I came in second place.

“What’s that kid's name, Roc?”

“Who?”

“The kid that came in second on that one.”

“I’m not sure.”

Coach George walked over and pointed at me, “What’s your name, son?”

Nervous, I said the first thing that came to my mind.

“Doodles!”

"Doodles?" he said, furrowing his brow. "Is that your real name?"

“No, it’s Rashod. Rashod is my real name.”

“OK, get back on the line.”

Coach George shook his head and walked back to Coach Roc.

“What’s wrong, Coach George?”

“What ever happened to names like Mike, Earl, Ricky?”

Coach Roc laughed as Coach George continued to list common names. "Jacob, Thomas, Jimmy?! That boy better be a star with a name like Doodles."

We ran through drills for about another hour before practice ended. Before we left, Coach George told everyone to get in a line to gather our information.

I need your name, mother's name, father's name, and phone numbers. If they don't live together, I need both parents' phone numbers. I need to get consent from both parents."

Man, I can't get my dad's consent: He's in jail.

As I get closer to the paper, Coach George told me to spell my name. He wrote the name down and asked what my mother and father's names were.

"Linda and Daniel Coleman."

He wrote both names down and said, "Cool. They live together?"

I felt like the whole park went silent, awaiting my answer. How would he react, knowing my father was in jail? Would I be cut from the team because my father didn't have a phone number? Would I be cut because my father couldn't give consent for me to play?

"They — ummm — they don't live together."

"Who do you live with, son?"

"My mom. On Franklin Street."

"OK, where does your father live?"

"He — ummm — lives in Smyrna, I think?"

Coach George, sensing my hesitation, put one and one together and said, "Cool. Just put your mother's phone number down, and I'll see you tomorrow."

I felt a weight lift off my shoulders when he said, "I'll see you tomorrow." Because my father was in jail, I never knew when I would see him next. So for another man to genuinely want to see me the next day meant so much to me. It was the first time I felt value come from a male. As I waited for Casime to finish, I heard Coach George speaking to other kids about their home situations.

"You're Darlene's son? Tell her I said hi. We went to high school together. That's my girl, so I know I'm not going to have any trouble out of you."

He made it such a loving environment for all of us young African American kids without active fathers.

Two days later, he gave out the list of everyone that made the team. Casime was able to get one of the papers and quickly found his name. As we searched for my name, I didn't see it. Heartbroken, I couldn't understand why. How did I not make the team? As tears began to well up in my eyes, another player asked, “Did you look at the other list? It’s in alphabetical order.”

We rushed over to the other paper. And there it was:

(Rashod “Doodles” Coleman).

Following practice that day, I had never felt so good. When we got back to “the block” with all of our friends, we couldn’t wait to tell them we’d made the football team. I was especially excited because we’d done it without any help from a man. Still, in the back of my mind...

I wish my dad was here.

CHAPTER 7

FATHER FIGURE

Kenneth, known around the neighborhood as K-Dog, eventually moved into the house with us. He would always invite me to come to my mother's room and watch the football game with him. I didn't know what being a son to a father was like, but when he would ask me to watch the game, for the first time, I felt like someone's son. During the games, I couldn't believe how intense he would get. It was weird because he was a Philadelphia Eagles fan, but he hated that they couldn't win a Superbowl. The only time he would root against them is when they would play the 49ers with Jerry Rice. Whenever Jerry Rice would score a touchdown, he would pick me up like a ragdoll and throw me across the bed; my mother, laughing in the background. I would always root for the other team in front of Kenneth because I knew when his team started winning, he would throw me. Those were some good times.

Throughout the years, K-Dog had struggled with substance abuse, but he never brought anything into our house. When I would see him outside of the house, he would always give me quarters and dollars. Though I knew he dealt with illegal narcotics, to this day, I have never seen him with drugs. A couple of my friends used to tell me that he sold and consumed drugs, but it was all foreign to me. He may have sold drugs, but he had also held down a job as a chef for a long time. Every time he came home, he would bring me some Starbursts from his job. When I would see him hanging with his boys on the street corner, he would always break away from them and toss the football with me. He was like a human encyclopedia when it came to anything that had to do with sports. He could tell where any NFL player was from, where they went to college, and what number they were picked in the draft. He could also talk to any and everyone. No matter if you were white, black, rich, poor, ghetto, or suburbians, he could have a good conversation with you.

"As long as you can communicate with people, you can get what you want." Those were just some of the rare gems he would impart to me when we were alone together.

One day, I came home wanting to play some football before practice, but I couldn't find Kenneth. I asked my mom if she saw him, but she said she hadn't. The news came on the television, and she quickly turned it off, which I thought was weird, but I really didn't think anything of it. He and my mom would often break up, so it was normal for him to leave days at a time. When they would break up, I would see him on the street corner, and he would always ask if everything was OK in the house as if he was still living there. A couple days later, I walked around to the street corner he hung at because I wanted to talk to him about Jerry Rice's game, but he wasn't out there as usual. When I got home that night, I asked my mom if she saw him and she said she hadn't.

A couple of days later, my mother sat my brother and me on the couch and said there was something she needed to tell us. Being a tight-knit family, I knew it had to be something big. I automatically said, "Are you pregnant?" to which she asked if I were crazy.

She said, "Kenneth got hurt pretty bad a couple of days ago. The story was all over the news, and I didn't want you guys to see it on there. He was stabbed by Big Mike." Big Mike was someone that I knew from around the neighborhood. "He just got out of his third surgery yesterday. So we might be able to go and see him tomorrow."

I left the room so hurt. Kenneth was the second man I knew after Roger, and here I was almost losing him too. Later that night, I went to my cousins' house — who were actually Kenneth's nephews — and they were also upset. They were not only upset because something happened to Kenneth but also Big Mike was their uncle on their mother's side. (Kenneth was their uncle on their father's side.) Big Mike got arrested for the attempted murder of Kenneth. That night, Jerry Rice was in a playoff game, and I felt like crying, watching him score a touchdown. I knew that after he scored a touchdown, Kenneth would pick me up and throw me across the bed. But instead, he was in the hospital fighting for his life.

The next day, my mother took us to Christiana Hospital. We stood outside Kenneth's room, waiting for the nurse to allow us to go in. When we finally went into the room, I didn't recognize Kenneth. It was a man with all of these tubes running throughout his mouth and chest. He couldn't speak, but he squeezed my hand as I stood there, an 11-year-old boy, watching him fight for his life. As I sat there wondering what state he was in, the nurse said, "You are allowed to talk to him. He can hear you." Kenneth's eyes opened and turned to me as I said, "Jerry Rice scored two touchdowns last night. Did you see the game?"

He shook his head "no," as his eyes began to well up with tears.

"I'll let you know what happens next game, OK?" He nodded slightly as my mother told me it was time to go and that Kenneth needed rest.

About a month later, Kenneth got out of the hospital and came to stay with us. He showed me his chest, which had a big cross scar. He told me that he and Big Mike had gotten into an argument and that Big Mike had pulled out a knife and stabbed him right in the heart. The surgeons had to do open heart surgery on him several times. What amazed me is what Kenneth said next:

"When I was lying on the ground, I heard the medics pull up. As the EMTs stared at me, I had an out-of-body experience. I looked down at myself on the ground with the medics trying to figure out if I was alive or dead. They decided to put me in a body bag, signaling that I was too far gone. I remember asking God if I could have one more chance. I said, 'Please, God. Please. Just give me one more chance, and I will try my best to do right.' At that point, I went back into my body and began coughing. They opened the bag up and started CPR on me. I really felt that God gave me one more chance for a reason. I'm done with drugs, Rashod. I'm trying to do right from here on out. I don't know what that looks like because the streets are all I know, but I'm going to try."

Not long after, K-Dog and my mother got married. Eventually, they separated and got divorced. Till this day, K-Dog and I are good friends. It's not because he was the best thing that ever happened to our family — but because he was one of the best men in my life. We were living amongst wolves, and Kenneth knew how to navigate. He wasn't the biggest or the baddest person in the neighborhood, but he was definitely one of the smartest. He would tell me who I should and shouldn't be hanging with, and when to go home, always encouraging me to do right in school and continue playing sports. Though he left our family like Roger and my father, the things he taught me would serve as a guide later in life and help me raise my children. And for that, K-Dog will always be my main man.

CHAPTER 8

CASIME AND DOODLES

Throughout our football practices with the Redskins, Casime quickly rose to the starting quarterback position, and I became one of the starting receivers. We had an excellent running back who'd played the year before, named Gentris. Gentris was a heavyset kid, one year older than the rest of us but a beast at running back. He was the first player in little league I ever saw use a stiff jab.

"That stiff jab always gets Gentris an extra 4–5 yards," Coach George used to say.

Coach George and Gentris had a bond like no one else on the team. Coach loved Gentris but often yelled at him for not "hitting the hole" hard enough. "Hitting the hole" meant running as fast as possible to the hole the offensive line made for you during a running play.

Coach George would yell to Casime, "Line it up and run 22 Dive, Casime!"

Casime, the quarterback, would get the ball from the center and hand off to Gentris, who would run through a hole located between the center and guard.

Casime would begin in his high-pitched, prepubescent voice, "Ready? Set. Go!"

As the play developed, Coach George would quickly blow the whistle and yell at Gentris.

"Gentris, awww! My Jesus. Move out the way. Move out the

way."

He would hand the play call sheet to Coach Roc, who would smirk because he knew what was coming. Coach George would then take the whistle around his neck and swing it behind him, so the whistle was still around his neck but on his back. He would turn his Redskins hat backwards and line up behind the fullback in the backfield.

"Run it, Casime."

Gentris would sit on the sideline, embarrassed the coach had snatched him out.

"Ready? Set. Go!"

Though Coach George would start a little early, he got to the whole right when the fullback got there. Coach would push the fullback through the hole, making a couple moves on the linebackers and defensive backs. Everyone would burst out laughing at the coach, weighing about 300 lbs. — but with moves like Barry Saunders. Gentris understood Coach only wanted the best for him, as Coach did all of us.

The first game came, and we were scheduled to play against the Steelers. We were locked in a dog fight at halftime, with neither team putting any points on the board.

I looked up and saw my mom in the crowd, who had such a proud look on her face. During the third quarter, the Steelers hit us with a quick touchdown while missing the extra point. Gentris was having a good game running the ball, but every time we came close to scoring, they tightened their defense and focused on him. With about two minutes left on the clock, we were down by six points but driving. From the 50-yard line, Coach called 22 Dive, and Gentris hit the hole, which got us down to the 15-yard line. We ran three plays from the 15, but the other team's defense was just too tough. Coach George called timeout and trotted onto the field for this 4th & 10 play from the 15.

I was daydreaming, looking to the crowd to see where my mom was as he began talking.

"Look, guys, it's your time. We have to do it right now. We are going to run 22 Slant to Doodles on one."

As Coach George pointed his finger at me and said, "Doodles," I snapped back to reality.

Damn, that's me.

"Doodles, can you catch it?"

"Yes, sir," I said in a mumble because I still had a mouthpiece in.

Coach trotted off of the field, and Casime leaned into the huddle.

"22 Slant on one. Ready? Break."

I ran to the right side of the field as nervous as ever. Until this point, I hadn't caught a pass all day. I looked at the cornerback, tasked to stick me, and I could see he was just as nervous as I was. Was this my time? Was this the time I would prove I was a pretty good football player?

I could only think of what the coach used to tell me: "Run three yards, then turn left and catch the ball."

Jerry Rice, my favorite player, used to score off the slant play all the time, so the play call was perfect. I just needed to make sure I did what I was supposed to do and catch the ball.

Casime started, "Ready? Set. Go."

I began running, and before I knew it, I hit five yards. I forgot to turn left at three. Hopefully, it wasn't too late, but I knew the coach was going to yell at me. I was so excited, I forgot all about it. At five yards, I turned left and saw that Casime no longer had the ball. Out of the corner of my eye, I saw the ball headed in my direction.

Focus, Doodles, focus.

I closed my eyes and felt the ball hit my shoulder pads as I jumped in the air to brace for the impact. I landed on my feet, secured the ball, opened my eyes, and didn't see anyone in front of me. So I ran as fast as I could to the touchdown and saw the referee put his hands up.

"Touchdown! Nice catch, kid."

I had practiced my first touchdown celebration for years up to this point. I knelt down on one knee and said nothing. Complete silence from me as the crowd erupted. Moments later, my teammates came jumping on me to celebrate.

"Get in the huddle! Get in the Huddle!" Coach George yelled from the sideline."

I forgot we still had time for an extra point.

Casime came into the huddle to relay whatever coach told him on the sideline.

"22 Dive to Gentris on one. Ready? Break."

We all ran to line up.

"Ready? Set. Go."

I looked back from the receiver position, which I shouldn't have been doing, and saw Gentris hit the hole so quickly that he pushed the fullback through the hole as Coach George had done at practice.

Gentris now had the ball and ran toward the right corner of the endzone with one player to beat. The fast player hit Gentris at the four-yard line, which made Gentris stumble. Gentris gave him a stiff jab with his left hand, and the player fell to the ground. Gentris ran into the endzone, scoring the extra point. The crowd roared as he crossed the goal line. We all ran to meet Gentris in the endzone, while our coach walked across to the other team's coach to congratulate him.

After the game, we met in the endzone — all on one knee, to listen to the coach's post-game speech.

"We made a lot of mistakes, but you guys fought back. I'm so proud of y'all. Not necessarily because you won, but because you never gave up when they scored. That says a lot about our team this year. We have a lot of new guys that haven't been tested, and today was your test. Though it feels great to win, you're not always going to win, but you can always fight to win. No matter how bad things get, always fight to win. Now bring it in. One. Two. Three." And we all yelled, "Redskins!" We broke the huddle.

Coach George's words are truer now as a 37-year-old with three kids than ever before.

CHAPTER 9

VIRGIN?

My attraction to females has always been something that's on my mind. My first girlfriend was in kindergarten. It may seem like a young age, but it felt totally normal at the time. She was this light-skinned, long-haired girl named English. All the boys in the class liked her, but no one dared ask her out. Although I can't remember how I asked her to be my girlfriend, I remember how we broke up.

A kid in my class named Rob told me that she agreed to be his girlfriend, which was not OK with me. During our recess, as the whole class was playing, English climbed to the top of the sliding board to position herself to take a turn. While she was still at the top, I walked to the bottom and said, "Did you tell Rob you would be his girlfriend?"

She shrugged her shoulders and stayed silent.

"Yes or no?"

The whole class listened with anticipation. English stood there, staring at me.

"Look, you can have him," I shouted. "I'm not sharing my girl. I quit you!"

I stormed off and headed to the swing set. English and I never got back together. This would be the first of many relationships with females.

***

When it came to sex talks, our home wasn't what you would

typically think. Most fathers sit their sons down in an awkward moment and have a sweet, little conversation about "the birds and the bees." I've never had that talk, and until this day, I can't even tell you how "the birds and the bees" translates into sex. My father wasn't around, so there were no awkward moments to be had. My mother didn't have time to figure those things out working two — sometimes three — jobs. Mom had three boys who would all fight over talking on the phone to females, so I assume she knew physical intimacy was inevitable for us.

"Take these condoms and use them if you have sex," she would tell my brothers while cornering them as 16- and 17-year-olds. I was 12, but I can picture it like it was yesterday.

"If you get a girl pregnant now, it will alter your life forever. I made that mistake and don't want that for y'all," she said, passing them a brown paper bag filled with condoms.

She never gave me condoms; although, I'm sure she knew I was listening and taking mental notes. That was her way of dealing with awkward moments: Get straight to the point.

At the time, I was still a virgin. Most of my friends were older than I was and infatuated with sex the same way I was. My good friend Doc said he had sex in the fourth grade and was not shy about letting everyone know. It was like a badge of honor for boys. However, I was proud of being a virgin at the time, but I soon felt the peer pressure of having my first experience.

One day, Doc, Troy, and I sat on a stoop at the corner of Third and Broom street. Troy was about eighteen at the time, and Terrance and I were only twelve. A female in a short dress walked by us, and we all stared and drooled, which was the norm for us. After she was far enough that she couldn't hear our conversation, everyone chimed in about what they would do to her if she agreed to have sexual intercourse with us.

Troy said, "Man, I would hit that straight from the back. I don't even want to see your face," as he motioned like he had his hands around her hips, along with moving his hips back and forth.

Terrance and I laughed at him, acting like he was having sex with the woman who just walked by us.

"Nah, I'm going to let her ride me. I'm on some lazy stuff," Terrance chimed in. He then proceeded to show us by laying down on his back in the middle of the street with both legs straight out in front of him and his hands behind his head with his fingers crossed. Troy and I laughed so hard, our cheeks hurt.

My turn was next: "I'm going to pick her up in the air for three hours!" I motioned as if both of her legs were wrapped around me, moving my hips back and forth in an awkward jumping motion.

No one laughed, but Doc gave me a disgusted look as he always did before he would tell a joke.

"Three hours?! How the hell are you going to hold her up that long?" Terrance said.

I responded with, "I'm just kidding, I'm a virgin, man."

Terrance and Troy looked at each other, trying not to laugh. Then, unable to contain themselves, they ran up the block laughing as I stood there watching them go. Every ten feet, they would look back at me and start laughing harder. It wasn't that funny to me, but Doc had the kind of laugh that would make you laugh, so I began laughing with them.

They eventually walked back to me, wiping their eyes as if they were crying. Just when I thought it was over, Doc would start laughing and running to the corner again with Troy following behind him.

They eventually came back again and switched the subject, but I had never felt so small in my life. The damage was done. After that day, every time sex came up in a conversation, Doc would lie and say that I had had sex before — especially in front of our older friends. He would say he didn't want people thinking I'm a punk for being a virgin. That was Doc. He always knew how to get himself or other people out of awkward situations.

During that time, I couldn't see what was so good about having sex. I had masturbated a couple times in my room while watching the fuzzy channel 99 on our cable box. Channel 99 was the naughty channel that we didn't have in our television package, but every now and then, you could see what was going on. I wasted a half hour with no big boom at all. Later, I would understand that I had not gone through puberty yet or had a wet dream, so I was mostly wasting my time.

That year, I met a girl in school named Kendal. K, as I used to call her, had light skin, long hair, and thick glasses. She came to our school, HB DuPont Middle School, in the middle of the year. We began dating and would have these long passionate kisses on the bus every day. I was used to pecks, but she often stuck her tongue in my mouth while we kissed. We had discussions about having sex, and she revealed to me that she wasn't a virgin. I didn't pry more about when she lost her virginity because my friends, who were also twelve, had already lost theirs.

My first time going over to her house, it was raining outside. I took some condoms from my brother's drawer because we had talked about having sex that night. Her parents had this huge house on the other side of town. K met me at the door, and her mother greeted me in the living room. After some small talk, her very courteous mother went upstairs to her room. K looked in my eyes and asked if I was ready, to which I nodded and started kissing her neck.

She pushed me off and said, "Not here, silly. We are going downstairs."

She grabbed my hand and escorted me downstairs to her basement. The room was carpeted and had a long, brown leather couch in it — along with a matching recliner. They also had a large 55" TV on the wall. She told me to sit on the couch and that she would be right back. At that point, all I could hear was my mother's voice talking to my older brother about sex.

"Wear a condom if you have sex. Here, take these and always protect yourself. You don't want to catch a disease or have a baby." I touched my pocket and felt the outline of the condoms.

As a twelve-year-old getting ready to have my first sexual intercourse experience, I had so many questions I wanted to ask my father. "Is it going to hurt when we start? Am I supposed to say anything to her before we get started? Do I leave my clothes on and unzip, or take my clothes completely off?" I needed a father, but I had no one to speak to about this momentous moment. I was just winging it. If the streets taught me anything, it was to act like you've been there before. I wasn't scared or nervous. I felt like I was late to the party because all my friends were already ahead of the game and I wanted to catch up.

When she came back downstairs, I noticed that she had changed from jeans to sweatpants. She told me we had to wait a little while for her mother to close her bedroom door. Every fifteen minutes, she would run upstairs and check. Finally, after her fourth time checking, she said, "OK, we are good. Her door is closed."

I watched as she got undressed, mimicking her because I had no clue what I was doing. As she took off her shirt, I took mine off. Next, her pants came down, and I removed mine. All that was left was her underwear. As she reached for hers, I did the same. Both of our clothes were on the floor in a split second. She asked me what position I wanted, to which I shrugged my shoulders. She could tell I was nervous, and though I thought it was the man's job to take charge, she didn't have a problem accepting the lead role.

"I'll get on top," she said with a smile.

I laid down on the brown leather couch. K grabbed a pillow from the matching recliner across from us and put it under the back of my head as I laid back. Grabbing the remote to the television, which was playing Richie Rich, she turned up the volume. After putting the remote on the floor, she took her right index finger and lightly ran her finger from my forehead past my chin, neck, chest, left leg, down to my big toe. I was erect before she started doing that, but at the conclusion, IT was on a whole different level.

"Did you bring them?" she asked, referring to the condoms. I reached down with my left hand as my cold body lay on the leather couch and removed the condoms from the pocket of the jeans on the floor next to the sofa. I had practiced putting on the condom days prior, so at least I could do that part.

With both index fingers and thumbs, I pulled one of the rubbers, strong-smelling, latex condoms from the packet and put it on. While watching, K pinched the condom's tip, filled with air, to give room for ejaculation. As I laid back again, she opened another condom and slid it on top of the first. I closed my eyes awaiting heaven and heard the ruffling of another condom being opened. She put on a third and then a fourth. At this point, I could feel my heart beating faster and faster.

She climbed on top, positioning both of her knees on each side of my waist. Grabbing down between her legs, she positioned my erect penis directly in front of her vagina. She lowered herself down very slowly while giving off a quiet moan. I could feel that my penis was only halfway in, so I pushed upwards, and she tensed up and said, "Go slow. I don't want you to pop my cherry."

I had no clue what the hell she was talking about. I interpreted it to mean, "Be still and let me do all the work." I didn't have a problem with it. Doc popped in my mind, so I mimicked him lying in the street by placing both hands behind my head. She looked at me and said,

"You comfortable?"

"I'm good to go," I replied.

While on top, her movements were up and down as if she was riding a horse. With the four condoms, I couldn't feel a thing. At one point, I looked over and started watching the movie on the television. It was about an hour and a half after we started. The movie started again, and I was still lying there.

She eventually looked down at me and said,

"Did you cum yet?"

"Come where?" I said with a confused look.

"In your condom?"

She got up and looked at the four condoms on my erect penis and said, "You still haven't come? Have you had a wet dream yet?"

"Nah!" I replied.

We thought we heard someone walking upstairs, so we hurriedly put our clothes on and finished watching the movie. As I sat next to the girl who took my virginity, I realized I didn't feel any different from when I first sat down a virgin. The only exception was now Doc no longer had to lie for me.

The act, in itself, wasn't anything special to me at the time. Like most people, if I could go back, I would have saved that moment; but growing up too fast and wanting to do too much was just part of our lifestyle when you don't have a father. I wished there had been a man to tell me, "No, son, you're only twelve-years-old. Your whole life is ahead of you, and the distraction of satisfying these hormones at such a young age is terrible." But none of us had those kinds of conversations. Therefore, we continued to make uninformed decisions.

CHAPTER 10

SCARRED FOR LIFE

It was around 9 PM, and the doctor's office was closed. The office was quiet and very cold as I laid my body on the steel table to prepare for surgery. The doctor who was on emergency call rushed in the room and quickly numbed my forehead. I laid on the table a 13-year-old boy, and would soon sit up only to see tears in my mother's eyes, as she glanced up at my forehead. I turned to the mirror and what I saw was a stranger looking at me.

Seven hours earlier, I was your average city kid riding the school bus home. I often sat with my girlfriend in the front seat and whispered sweet nothings in her ear. This particular day, the clothes I had on were blue jeans, brown Columbia boots, a brown flannel shirt, and a colorful brown and blue knitted hat. The bus I rode home wasn't my assigned bus, but my good friend Jabbar, who was Lenny's cousin, and I would frequently ride this bus because not only were all of our guy friends on the bus but also HB DuPont's most beautiful middle school girls were too. Who could have ever predicted that the following events would change my appearance forever?

As I was sitting in the front seat, I think Deon took my hat off my head and quickly threw it to the back of the bus. It was a game we played all the time, and I can't say I didn't indulge when it was someone else's hat. As I laughed and looked to the back, everyone avoided eye contact while trying not to laugh. I looked into some of the leading corporates seats and didn't see it, so I decided to laugh it off and head back to my seat.

As the bus approached Lancaster Avenue and Route 141, someone shouted, "Carla has your hat."

I responded without looking back, "It's OK. I'll get it before I get off the bus."

Carla was someone I knew from the neighborhood, and though we didn't hang out with each other, I never saw her as a mean person. She was a year older than me, and older guys loved her because her physique was very mature, and she had a great personality, but I digress.

After Carla heard what I said, she replied, "I don't have your stinkin' ass hat!"

I then said in a harsher tone, "Bitch, you stink!"

That statement wasn't true, but it was all I could think of at the time.

Eventually, after yelling back and forth, she walked the entire length of the bus and attempted to hit me in the head with an umbrella. I blocked the umbrella, grabbed her by the collar, and shoved her to the bus's back. Moments later, she approached me again, but this time with a box-cutter in her hand. I realized what she had in her hand; I knew that this had gone too far.

With both hands in the air, I looked directly in the eyes and said, "What are you going to do-- cut me?"

She didn't answer with words. She didn't respond with constants and vowels. She didn't put a complete sentence together with subject-verb agreements. She raised the box cutter and cut me from the hairline on my head to a centimeter from my eyeball.

As I shockingly walked back to my seat, I could see by the expression on my classmate's faces that it was terrible. Blood gushing down my head and looking for something to stop the bleeding, guess what someone threw to me? MY HAT! With the hat turning bright red from the blood, I could only think of my future. Just entering my teenage years, there were already so many insecurities I would have to deal with, but this would be like no other.

She took something from me on that day. Something internal! The damage had been done, and I wouldn't come to understand it for years. I felt like the bird whose wings got cut before he left the nest. I felt like the Lion who never learned to hunt before being kicked out of the pride-or the vegetable crop that didn't get enough water to survive. The mother bird would eventually bring the food back. The Lion would subsequently learn his capabilities, and the rain that God provided would make up for lack of care by the farmer.

Similarly, I, too, with 52 stitches in my head, would stand tall again. But it scarred me. It scarred me for life.

CHAPTER 11

CONRAD STREET

Though this wasn't turning out to be the best year of my life, I still had all of my boys behind me. They looked out for me all the time, and I definitely looked out for them. Most of my friends were a little older but not by much. In the seventh grade, I was 13 years old, my boy Kev was 15, and Doc was 14. One night, while we were all hanging out on the street corner, one of the older drug dealers(That lived around our area named Big Will) came riding by in a new black car. The car had tinted windows, chrome rims, and looked like something from the future. When he stopped, we all walked up to the car to show our admiration. Kev jokingly asked when Big Will was going to let him drive the vehicle. Will said he had some business to take care of, but for us to meet him in about an hour on Conrad Street so that we could take the car for the night.

We all looked at each other as Big Will pulled off and behind talking about where we would go and who would drive when. Though T-doc and I were in middle school, we already had a lot of experience driving vehicles. T-Doc's uncle Ronnie was the first one to let us drive his car. Well, maybe he just let us listen to the radio in the parking lot, and we took it for a quick spin. After getting comfortable driving at 10 and 11 years old in the parking lot, we started asking some of our older friends to borrow their cars. The police in the neighborhood knew who drove what car, so everyone would switch cars and get "Bloop rides." A

"Bloop ride" was a drug addict's vehicle who didn't have any money but wanted to get high. He would lend people his car for a couple hours in exchange for a few dollars. It was similar to Enterprise — just on a street level. Those were the best kind of cars because the older guys didn't really care when we brought the car back. It was also dangerous because you were dealing with a drug addict, most of whom were not from our neighborhood. Sometimes, the proposition would sound good to them, but a couple hours later, they would get cold feet and report the vehicle stolen simply to get their vehicle back. They would never press charges which would upset the police, but it was all a part of the street culture.

Around 8:00 PM, we headed to Conrad Street to meet Big Will. Conrad Street was a notoriously busy drug block. There was a bar on the corner called Cat Paws, which everyone went to at the end of the night. That block was good for drug dealing because it was a small block with a bunch of alleyways that you could enter and exit out of at any time. There was no time of day that you went to that block, and it was empty. Though there was a lot of drug activity, there was not a whole lot of violence. Maybe someone drunk arguing with their partner, but other than that, people were about getting money down there. There is an old saying on the street, "You can't get money when it's hot, and violence brings police."

As we approached Will, he had a new pair of Jordan's on which we all complimented him. He simply threw us the keys and didn't even stop talking to someone that he was speaking with on his cellphone. Kev got in the driver's seat, I got in the passenger seat, Doc hopped in the back and we headed towards the North Side of Wilmington. The North Side was where all the cute girls our age were out all night. It was also the side of town where you wouldn't get shot or beat up because you were not from there. They were more of your pretty boys. We got a couple of the girls' numbers as we drove around and then headed back to take the car back to Big Will.

As we pulled up to Conrad Street, it was around 10:00 PM, and he was still sitting on the same step from when we left. We gave him the keys, had some small talk, then headed back towards Kev's house, which was straight up Third Street (Conrad Street runs parallel to 3rd Street). As we walked away from Will towards 3rd Street, Kevin said,

"Yo, I'm going to ask Will for a dollar, so I can get something to drink." We made a U-turn back towards Will, and Kevin began engaging in a conversation with him.

Out of nowhere...

POP POP, POP POP!

I looked to Will, who didn't say a word, just started running in the opposite direction of Third Street. We all took off behind him, ducking below the firing someone was doing in our direction. We could hear people screaming and crying as we continued to run.

Is this it for me?

Will my mom have enough money to pay for my funeral? She's already struggling, and because of my stupidity, and knowing this is a busy drug block, and still coming down here, I might never see her again, and it's my fault.

Luckily, we made it to Kev's and took off our shirts to make sure we weren't hit.

T-Doc said, "Yo, Kev. If we didn't make that U-turn and turn back to talk to Will, we would have walked right into the dude shooting."

I chimed in, "God was looking out for us, man. There had to be an angel, dawg. We were right there!"

That wasn't my first time seeing someone shooting, but it was the first time being around someone shooting and not knowing who the target was. I didn't know if the shooter was aiming at us, Big Will, or some random person out there. Either way, I knew I had to move differently. That was a close call, and I couldn't have my mom crying over my casket because I wanted to be cool and ride around talking to girls. I don't think anyone got hit that night, but I might not be so lucky next time. At that point, I had only been on this earth for 13 years. Can you imagine if that would have been it for me? I would work hard in the coming years to make sure it wasn't me, but it wouldn't be easy.

CHAPTER 12

I MADE MOM CRY

In the eighth grade, I decided to take a home economics class because there was cooking involved. For some reason, I thought we would bake chocolate chip cookies all day. Little did I know, I would be making pillows and pot warmers. Because the class wasn't turning out the way I had planned it, I spent most of my time talking to Shauna, who sat next to me. She was a short blond-haired tomboy who always hung out with the preppy white kids. One day she came in class, sat next to me, and said, "What do you think about Karen?"

Karen was a short white girl, who always wore tight bell-bottom pants with sketcher sneakers, and these cute brunette bangs in her hair. Up to this point, I don't even think I knew anyone in an interracial relationship, so it was the farthest thing from my mind. I spoke to her here and there, and I thought she was cute, but I didn't know if she liked black guys, which is always an issue. She lived in a town called Hockessin, one of the wealthiest areas in the state of Delaware. They had these huge houses and land everywhere in Hockessin. That's where our middle school was located, so we would have to take that hour trip every morning on the school bus. It was definitely on the other side of the tracks.

I told Shauna, "She seems cool. Why, wassup?"

As she sat to the left of me, she leaned over to me, hitting me with her right elbow and said, "Do you think she's cute, Doodles?"

I started smiling and rubbing my peach fuzz beard.

Huh. She is pretty cute...but, I'm not sure how my boys will look at me when I tell them I'm dating a white girl.

It might seem like a nonfactor now, but as an eighth-grader, it was a tough decision.

"She thinks you're cute." She said while tapping me with her elbow again.

That was probably the first time I'd heard those words since I got cut on my forehead a year before. I dealt with many insecurities because of my scar that I even stopped talking to girls for a while.

I guess I can say, "Those words swept me off my feet."

We became a thing pretty fast, and it was so different from dating a black girl. It wasn't better or worse, just extremely different. For example, my girlfriend last year was very athletic and extremely good at basketball. She couldn't beat me one-on-one, but she was probably the best female basketball player I knew. She could ride bikes, fight, and was very aggressive intimately.

Conversely, Karen was very laid back, loved to get her hair done, and hated playing sports. I would walk her to class all the time, which often made me late to mine.

At one point, my counselor, Mrs. Parks, called me into her office.

When I got there, the first thing she said was, "What's going on with you and Karen? Is she the reason you keep getting to class late?"

I started smiling and answered, "Of course not, Mrs. Parks!"

She smiled back at me, then proceeded to lean back into her seat while taking her glasses off and placing them on her desk.

"Doodles, why are you smiling so hard? I only asked you one question."

I sarcastically answered, "Me, smiling? Nah, I'm chilling." Then I proceeded to lean back in my chair, mimicking her posture.

"Your nose is wide open, Mr. Coleman."

Being an eighth-grader and not understanding what that term referred to, I asked, "What does that mean?"

"Are you in love, Doodles?"

I grabbed one of the pins off her desk and pretended to be looking at it during our awkward silence. "Yeah, I'm in love."

"You're an eighth-grader. What do you know about love? What is love, Mr. Coleman?"

"It's when you respect each other. Karen respects me, and I respect her."

"OK, Doodles!" She said while raising her eyebrows and widening her eyes while looking down at her desk. "Have you guys talked to your parents about this relationship?"

I thought about it and said, "No, not yet."

When I got home that night, my mother was in her bedroom watching a television show and doing her hair. I walked into the room to speak with her.

"Hey, mom, what up?"

"Nothing, son. How was school today?"

"It was cool. I spoke with Mrs. Parks today."

"Oh, that's my girl. What is she talking about?"

"Nothing much. I got a new girlfriend at school."

She stopped doing her hair, pushed mute on the television, and turned her attention towards me. I could no longer hold my smile in, so I started laughing.

"She must be cute because you're smiling from ear to ear."

"Yeah, she's cute. Hopefully, you will meet her soon."

"I hope so. She has my son smiling from ear to ear. Where does she live?"

"Out by the school. In Hockessin."

My mom worked not far from school, so she was familiar with the area. She stopped doing her hair again. "She lives in Hockessin."

"Yeah, She's white."

Her eyes dropped to the ground, and she put everything down that she was using on her hair. She picked her eyes back up from the ground and looked at me for an awkward silent three seconds.

"Doodles, are you just playing with me?"

"About what?"

"You are dating a white girl?" In a raised tone.

"What are you upset about? You know what? Nevermind." I stormed out of her room.

"Get your ass back here," she yelled into the hallway at me.

I came back to the threshold of her door and stared in the air, uninterested about what she was going to say next. I finally have a girl I like, and my mother is not happy because she is a white girl? That's just ridiculous.

She had both of her elbows on her knees with her fingers interlocked behind her head.

I could only think, *what the hell is wrong with this woman? Did Mrs. Parks know that she was going to react like this?*

She didn't look up at me. She just said, "Doodles sit down."

I walked into the bedroom and sat on the side of the bed behind her.

She turned back with tears swelling up in her eyes. At that point, I couldn't believe I had done something to make my mother cry. She was the person who was the centerpiece of our small family, and I made her cry. I felt terrible at this point, but maybe if she saw how sweet Karen was, she wouldn't be so upset. I didn't feel like I said anything that bad, but apparently, I did.

She began, "Doodles, your father."

What does this have to do with my father? What is wrong with my mother right now?

"Your father. He um, I know you don't know a lot about why he is in jail. He was accused of kidnapping a white woman and sexually assaulting her. She lied on him. The white police officers that arrested him lied on him, and the district attorney lied on him. They gave him life, Rashod, Life!"

"But, but..."

"But Nothing Doodles. I've seen the way white people treated your father. I don't want you going down this path. Please Doodles. Please!"

I walked out of the room, and I didn't know what to think. My father was serving a life sentence, so that means he is never getting out of that place? Karen isn't like whoever that woman is, that lied on my father. She would never do anything like that to me. I had so many questions about my father's case at that point. Did he have a girlfriend that was white? Is he just claiming that he didn't do it, but he did? Within a couple of months, I liked this white girl, yet maybe I would have to put those feelings aside. No matter how much I liked her, I loved my mother, and I hated to see her cry.

CHAPTER 13

SENIOR YEAR

By my senior year, I was one of the top recruits in Delaware when it came to football. I received letters from every big-name school in the nation. Notre Dame, Miami University, Florida State, USC, and a plethora of other schools. Some had my name on the recruiting letter, and some said dear recruit. Dear recruit, usually meant they didn't really know who you were but wanted to keep you in the loop.

My head football Coach, Coordie Greenlea, was this hardnose coach who went to college in Delaware but was from upstate New York. I say hard nose because no matter how good or bad things were, no matter how good or bad of a player you were, no matter what the situation was, he wanted you doing the right thing. If you wanted to do the wrong thing, he had a problem with you. And with the stature of a Division I Center, he had the ability and physical presence to make you think twice about testing him. Every now and then, players tested him and one Thursday practice he would show who's boss.

On this sunny afternoon, our best linemen Ray was having a bad day, and the coaches didn't appreciate him going half-speed through his drills. After being corrected one too many times, Ray snapped!

"I'm out of here," Ray said as he walked out of practice. Ray was no pushover standing at about 6'1", 250 pounds of all muscle.

“Take your lazy behind to the locker room,” Coach Greenlea

said, as Ray walked towards the school to exit the practice. After Ray heard the coach say that, he stopped in his tracks and turned around as everyone, players and coaches, stopped to see what Ray was going to say.

"You want to fight?" Ray yelled from a small hill, right before the pavement.

Coach responded, "Boy, you better go ahead."

Ray threw his helmet down and went on a full sprint straight towards Coach Greenlea. We all stood there watching how this was going to play out.

As Ray ran from about 20-yards away in a direct line to coach, my eyes panned to the coach who had his whistle in his mouth and a play calling paper in his right hand. As Ray got five feet away from him, Coach Greenlea gave a quick squat to brace for impact, slightly turned his body to the right so Ray would hit his right shoulder and caught Ray with a mean forearm right to the throat. We all stood there amazed as the situation unfolded Ray left practice but returned the next day and were back to business as usual.

During my ninth-grade year, after failing a math test, Coach Greenlea pulled me in his office and chewed me out.

"I can't depend on you if you fail off the team." Those words hit me hard because no man, especially no black man has ever said he depended on me for anything, so hearing those words meant a lot to me. Though I didn't learn as much as I should have in high school, I definitely didn't want to let him down. He depended on me for something, and though it might have been small to him, it was huge to me.

After one of my basketball practices, during my sophomore year, I saw him in the locker room, and he called me over to talk to him.

"What do you want to do for college? Where do you want to go?"

College? I thought to myself. Coach must not know my background. My mother is a single woman with two other sons. My father is serving life, and I don't even know anyone in my family that has been to college. We don't have the finances, nor do we even know what the first step is to do something like that. I'm from 3rd and Broom Street, and people from that place never go to college. We grow up, become drug dealers, and hold our block down. That's just how it goes.

"College? I don't know about that, Coach."

"What you mean? I think you're good enough to play."

"Really?"

"Yeah, your 40-yard dash times are good, you can catch, and you're strong. Why not?"

"That's all good, but my mom doesn't have money to be wasting on me."

"Wasting? It's an investment, but she won't even have to pay for anything. They have financial aid and scholarships that help you pay for it."

"Really?"

"Yeah, man. It's nothing for you out there on that street corner. You're better than that."

I walked away really believing those words. Maybe I was better than that block. Maybe I could be something other than a drug dealer. My dad was doing life, my brothers had been locked up, so why am I so special that I can do something different? How will people look at me when I tell them I'm thinking about leaving the block and heading to college? Coach struck a match in me, and I can't disappoint him.

CHAPTER 14

COLLEGE DAYS

If you would have asked me during my ninth- and tenth-grade years in high school, if I was going to college, it would have been a definite, "No." After my high school football coaches, Greenlea and Ryan began shaping my mind and classes for college, I was locked in. My mother and stepfather dropped me off at Delaware State University (Conwell Hall, room 235) which would be my residents for my first year. Because my grades and SAT scores were not up to par during my high school years, I had to sit out from playing football during my first year of college. It turned out to be one of the best things for me.

During my freshman year at Delaware State University, I was considered a "Prop-48," a player who didn't have the grades to play the first year but could work out and condition as a group. I became close with a guy named Ernest, whose nickname was EJ. He and I quickly became friends because both of us came from tough backgrounds. I came from avoiding drugs and guns. My mother's fear was me becoming a drug dealer and caught up in the streets. Ernest, who came from southern Delaware, struggled to keep the light and water on which I couldn't fathom. I was thinking that I would live the toughest life ever because I was raised without a father, but Ernest's family worked hard, and it was still a struggle. Ernest lost his father to sickness when he was only 16-years-old. Going to visit his family on a free weekend, I was amazed to see trailer parks and wells with water coming out of them. I really appreciated his struggle and his mother's grit to keep her focused and give her children a chance at the American Dream. She would always show me so much love when I would go down to visit her. To this day, I call her my adopted mother. Hey Liby!

Though I had a support group that was in the same position as me, I still kind of felt like an outcast. I had left all my boys from back home and searched for a better life, and though it's a good thing now, at the time, it felt selfish. I felt this way for the first couple of weeks of school until I went to my first concert.

There was buzz going around campus about this new up and coming rapper coming to perform at our school. It was hard for me to believe that 50 Cent was coming for a Valentine's Day concert. He had just dropped his hit album "Get Rich or Die Trying," and everyone was talking about him. I thought to myself, *there is no way this guy is coming*. On the day of the concert, I bought a ticket because even if 50 wasn't going to be there, there were females that would be there, and I wasn't going to miss that. We all packed into the gymnasium, where the party was on at 10:00 PM. The Lights were low, and all the girls were in there dancing. EJ and I were next to each other, dancing with every girl that attempted to walk by, which was our MO. Suddenly, the DJ said, "I think it's time to put my G-Unit shirt on."

The light popped on. Lloyd Banks and Young Buck (who were part of 50 Cent's group), came on stage and said, "When I say 50, y'all say Cent...50!"

"Cent!"

"50!"

"Cent!"

"When I say G, y'all say Unit. G!"

"Unit!"

"G!"

"Unit!"

And running up the steps was Curtis Jackson, AKA 50 Cent. Before I knew it, EJ and I were in the front row with the screaming girls singing every song word for word. As I went back to my room after the concert, I knew college was for me.

CHAPTER 15

RELATIONSHIPS

Delaware State was considered a Historically Black College / University (HBCU). I had just come out of high school where now that I think about it, I went against my mother's wishes and dated white girls the whole time. The first girl I had a serious relationship with in college was a girl named Tasha. She was this cute, light-skinned girl I had been chasing around for a year. She refused to give me the time of day or even her number, but eventually, she came around. Usually, with women, I'm captivated by looks, and she was cute as ever, but what I loved about her was her intellect. She was so smart in the classroom. I couldn't believe she was Black and getting A's in every class she took. I know that's such an ignorant statement, but I guess my mind was just not that mature at the time. She would help with my schoolwork and show me how to schedule my classes so I could graduate.

At that particular time, I just knew this was the girl for me. She would talk to me about the Bible and certain scriptures that I had never seen before. She said her father was a pastor and that I should go to meet him sometime in her hometown in Haveloc, North Carolina. Though we talked a lot of church stuff and her father was a pastor, we had sex almost every night. They say college was the time for exploration, and we definitely explored.

On a summer break, I decided to travel with her to see her father. From all accounts, he seemed like a good dude from talking to him on the phone, so I was eager to meet him. I also used it as a time to stay faithful to her. Though I was captivated by her, I was still cheating on her with other girls. I thought that maybe if I could meet her family and get to know her a little better, I would slow down on some of the side relationships I was having.

When we got to her house in North Carolina, her family could not have been more hospitable. When I arrived at her hometown, they took me in as if we had been together for 20 years. I loved seeing a family where the Black father was the head. My father had always been absent, so their family dynamic was foreign. He drove me around, showed me the city, and then we began talking about his daughter. I told him that I cared about her, but I didn't know what the future held. He then responded by telling me he would give me money to buy her a ring and that I needed to get serious and stop playing. Maybe he smelled the BS on me, but I didn't feel that was how he should have gone about it. That really turned me off about this trip. After that conversation, I sort of felt that it was a ploy by her to hurry up and get down the aisle. I think she would have been a great wife, but at that point, I was no man. I had the stature of a man, but my mind was still childish, and that would have been a disaster.

She eventually came to my hometown to meet my family. My mother and grandmother, who are big in the Church, fell in love with her. And how could they not? She was pretty, smart, and loved to be around Church people. A year after we visited my hometown, she and I began to have problems mainly with my infidelities. Though we had broken up, we were still having sexual relations, and I was doing what many 20-year-old men do on the side. I knew it was wrong, but I thought it was just what guys do. It was what I was used to doing. We stayed in touch for a while, but eventually, we both decided to part ways, and I think that was one of the best decisions we ever made.

After college, EJ and I got an apartment together in Newark, Delaware. I was fresh out of a relationship, and he was single, so you can only imagine the traffic coming through that place. Happy hour every Friday and parties every Saturday. Jeez! What an expensive time. At one happy hour, we went to this hole-in-the-wall bar called My Place, next to our apartment complex. There were a bunch of people there, the majority of whom were Black people, with two white girls. Who do I end up talking to by the end of the night? One of the white girls.

Her name was Jennifer. A tall, blond-haired woman with a cute smile. She had a very soft voice but was extremely quick on her feet when it came to sarcasm, which is what I liked about her. She told me she lived in Rehoboth

Beach, which I thought was just a vacation spot. I didn't know that people actually live there. We talked on the phone and texted a lot, but when we saw each other, our sexual chemistry was like no other. Every time we were physically intimate, we had to change sheets. We would literally drive almost two hours just to see each other, then drive back.

She was an overall great girl to be around. We would argue a lot about dumb stuff, but for the most part, I thought we got along pretty well. She knew I loved the Eagles, so she took me to an Eagles and Ravens game, which up until then was one of the nicest things anyone has ever done for me. It wasn't the fact that it was expensive. It was that throughout the day, she just said she was enjoying me having a great time. My heart melted for her after that trip. I guess because of my father, I had always felt abandoned, and this was a time in my life where I felt like someone really cared about my happiness.

Months later, while I was in her condo, waiting for her to get off work, I decided to get on her laptop. I would be lying if I said I wasn't snooping. On the laptop, inside of her picture, I saw another guy that she took to a football game. Like me, this guy looked like he was having the time of his life. I was so hurt after viewing those pictures that my stomach hurt. I didn't eat dinner that night, and we didn't even have sex; it was so bad. She told me she didn't know where we stood, so she was just, "Doing her." She broke my heart that night. And truth be told I wasn't faithful to her, we didn't have a conversation about girlfriend/boyfriend, but for some reason, after that football game, she was all I could think of for a while. I even contemplated where I would work if I were to move down there with her.

I wish I could say that's where our troubles ended, but it wasn't. It was something about having my heart broken like that that I couldn't let go. Shamefully, I contacted one of her good friends via social media. We got together at night for drinks and mainly talked about Jennifer. My conscious was killing me all night knowing I shouldn't be there and that surely this wasn't the way to pay someone back, but at the time, I didn't care. She didn't know how bad she hurt me by taking another dude to do this thing I felt took me not only to another level in our relationship but also in my life. I was crushed to know that the one person I thought cared for me was doing the same thing with someone else. As her friend and I flirted and talked, she complimented me on my cologne.

I told her that "Jennifer bought it for my birthday!"

She became outraged and said she knew she had smelled that scent before. She also said that she bought that same cologne for her ex-boyfriend that Jennifer slept with. I was done at that point. Any reservations about turning back were long out the window, and we finished the night with doing what grown people do. And the only way I knew how to get people back was to fight fire with fire.

To this day, I am truly ashamed of my actions, but I own it. I was a man; I knew what I was doing, and I am truly, truly sorry!

CHAPTER 16

A BREATH OF FRESH AIR

When Jennifer and I were still seeing each other, I offered her to accompany me to an end of the year party at my co-worker Kelly's house. It was such a good night of drinking and introducing her to all of my co-workers, including this one cute one named Amy.

Amy was a Church girl. I had never seen Amy with a boyfriend, but there were definitely a lot of guys attempting to spark a relationship with her. I really paid her no mind because I didn't know if she found black men attractive or not. Also, I already had too much going on with Jennifer, so I wasn't interested in fighting over one co-worker. Towards the end of the night, I saw across the room that Amy was upside down with two of our male co-workers holding each leg in the air. Apparently, this is what white people call an upside-down keg stand. To say the least, I was impressed. I left the party early with Jennifer, and we stayed the night at my place.

The following year, during another happy hour, Amy and I got into an argument about a student that we both taught. The kid was rough around the edges and played a lot of games in the classroom, which disrupted teachers, but he was like so many friends I had, who were given up on. My plea to her was that the kid needed more chances. I wasn't making that argument because I thought he would get better any time soon for her, but because one day, he would look back and appreciate the teachers who gave him chance after chance. She wasn't having it. She was done with him and all the antics that he would pull in her class. Throwing her erasers and markers in the trash so that she couldn't find them was just too much for her. We both left that discussion, probably not feeling the greatest about each other, but we did get the chance to express ourselves.

At the end of this school year, the whole staff got together and played an old Italian game of Bocci. During the game, I commented on a couple of her throws to which she gave me some of my own medicine when it was my turn. We eventually found ourselves talking alone as everyone else went inside the building to cool down. As I spoke with her, I noticed her eyes were different colors, and her smile was so, so cute. Eventually, we exchanged numbers and began texting every day. I offered to take her to the movies, and she rejected me saying she had to help her friend Beth paint. Even though we didn't get to the movies after she finished painting, she met me at one of our co-worker's houses, and the rest was history.

She was so calm all the time, and it helped that she laughed at my corny jokes. She told me she was homeschooled, which I didn't even know was a real thing at the time. We spoke of marriage and the future. Ironically, we were on the same page about how many kids we wanted and what that structure looked like after we had them. I told her that because my father has been locked up all my life, it pained me that my mother was forced to work so hard. I also let her know that I wanted to be the kind of husband that could allow my wife to stay home and not work if that's what she wanted. She explained to me that her mother stayed home, and it was something she always wanted to do also.

During that summer we spent a lot of time getting to know each other. Though I was talking to other females, I began putting all the relationships to rest. Though we were not having sex, she fulfilled what I needed mentally at the time, so sex was not a priority to me, and to this day, it feels funny saying that. All my life, at least since the 7th grade when I lost my virginity, sex has been something that has run my life. However, because of this relationship, I started to gain control.

CHAPTER 17

SEEKING APPROVAL

By this time, I had visited Amy's parent's house for Sunday dinners all summer long. I could tell that she wanted me to see who she really was. She showed me old pictures from when she was a skinny teenager with thick bright red glasses and a long braided ponytail down the middle of her back. She looked like a nerd, but I thought *man I want to marry this girl*. Amy introduced me to her eight siblings, which included five brothers and three sisters. I could tell she enjoyed cracking jokes, singing songs, and being around her family.

Before I would take the leap of asking her to marry me, It was also important that she meet both of my parents. There I was, a 26-year-old man who felt like I needed approval from my mother and father that I barely knew. I stopped by my mother's house one day after leaving one of Amy's family dinners to see if my mom would accompany next week to meet Amy's parents.

"Nah!" My mother said with a smile on her face.

"Why not, mom?" To be honest, I knew why. White people had torn my family apart, and to make matters worse, Amy's family lived in Newark; the same police department that arrested my father over 20 years ago.

"Pleeeeaaassseee, Mom?"

"Why do I need to go over there? Those are your people!"

"Haha, Mom. Haha!" I said sarcastically.

"Why do I need to go?"

"Because I want them to see who the number one woman in my life is. I want them to meet the best woman in the whole entire world," as I pulled her in for a strong bear hug and jokingly acted as if I were crying.

Reluctantly, she said, "OK. Whatever. What do I need to bring — some apple pie?"

"Just that beautiful smile, mom." I pulled her towards me for another bearhug.

"Oh, what's my dad's State Bureau Identification number, mom?"

"You're planning on writing to your father?"

"Nah, I'm going to take Amy to see him."

"Oooook!" she said, rolling her eyes.

"What do you think he's going to say, mom?"

"Your father is a man of few words. He will be happy you guys came to see him."

Really? I thought to myself. I don't even know why I felt the need to take my girlfriend to see him. I guess something in me was changing, now that I was thinking about marriage and having a family. I wanted her to truly know who I was. What ran inside my DNA, unfortunately, included a father who was serving life in prison.

I scheduled a visit with the prison to see my father the next day, which was Monday. Prison visits had to be scheduled no earlier than 72 hours and only Wednesdays. I confirmed for the Wednesday after next. When I told my girlfriend Amy we were going to see my dad, she didn't seem bothered by going into a jail for the first time. However, I knew whenever she gave a quick answer and did not have any questions, she was the most concerned and nervous. I think a part of her knew that I came from the "other side of the tracks," and she needed to play that "tough girlfriend role." Maybe it was to impress my friends or me, but the truth was, I was falling deeply in love with everything about this girl. So, it didn't matter what role she chose to play.

On the morning of the visit, Amy and I met at her house. She told me that she was frustrated because she couldn't figure out what to wear.

"You just can't wear anything tight or revealing," I told her.

She put on a gray T-shirt, blue jeans, and brown moccasin sneakers.

"OK. How does this look?"

"Looks great," I said without looking. I wasn't worried about what she wore, because one of the things I've always admired about her clothing was her modesty.

We drove her 1995 brown Honda Accord, and it took us about a half-hour before we arrived at Smyrna Prison. *There it is again,* I thought to myself, *those weird looking fences.* It's been almost 20 years since I've stepped foot into this place, but it was as if time had stopped. The doors, the paint, and the smells seemed the exact same, from the first time I went there as a four-year-old.

As we walked into the door, I had Amy take a seat on the same blue chair I had sat on almost 26-years-ago. I walked up to the man in the uniform and shiny badge (which I know now is a Correctional Officer) and presented my identification along with Amy's. He gave us two badges to pin on ourselves. When I returned to Amy, I sat in the seat to the right of her. She pinned the badge on and grabbed my left hand with her right hand. I looked her in the eyes and could see the nervousness. She couldn't hide it anymore. I don't care who it is, no one is prepared to walk into jail, and be locked in for the first time. I wanted to ease her nervousness, so I asked,

"You good, babe?"

"Yeah, I'm OK. Are you OK?

I looked around at the walls and said, “I don’t like coming into this place. I remember being a child coming in here. This is no place for people to live.”

“Does your dad look like you?”

"Nah. He's some light-skinned dude. If I didn't know any better, I wouldn't think he's my father. But we have the same ears and facial structure, I think. He has a lighter complexion."

I began looking around the room at the other families. They were all waiting to enter the facilities secured area to visit their loved ones. I made eye contact with one of the inmates wearing a white jumpsuit cleaning the room. It’s the same look from years ago. Not happy, not sad, just here. Just serving his time. I looked over to an African American mother and what looks like her son sitting across from us. He’s so short his feet can barely hit the floor. He’s around the same age I was when I first went to see my father. I had so many questions I wanted to ask that kid as he sat there with the familiar scared stare I once had. The same look I had when I first entered the jail as a four-year-old. *Do you know what you are about to go through having a father in prison? Do you know the pain that your mother is feeling and will feel until your father is released? Do you know that the life you are living right now is not normal? Do you know that none of this, and I mean none of this is your fault, but one day you will feel like it is? Do you know you are locked up too? Yes, you, as a 4-year-old, have to serve a life sentence as well.*

One of the Guards walked into the waiting area with the visitors and yelled, "Line it up!"

I explained to Amy that we had to go through the metal detector before going inside the secured area. There would be some loud noises, so she shouldn't be alarmed. I was attempting to keep her calm, but truth be told, I was scared, too. Though guards were around, something can still happen to you or the person you're accompanying at a visitation. When you ultimately make it to the visiting room, there is no barrier between you and the other inmates.

We walked through the metal detector with no problem, and all of a sudden: "EEEEEHHHH!" Amy nearly jumped out of her shoes. "I told you the alarm was going to go off," I smiled.

They herded us through a couple sections until we landed in the waiting room. This room was different from the last time I went to this jail. This room had a square brick wall that stood about four-foot-high in the center of the room. There were two visitor chairs every couple of feet on the outside of the wall. Then one chair inside of the wall facing the chairs on the outside of the wall. We took a seat to the left as we walked into the room and patiently waited.

I looked around the room at all the families and, in particular, the little guy from the waiting room. I couldn't actually see him because he was so short, but I saw his mom. I wished I could ask her questions. *Do you know what this young man will go through the rest of his life having a father incarcerated? How are you going to help him navigate living in this world without his father? Is there a plan laid out for other men to mentor this young man?*

In the midst of my daydreaming...

EEEEEH!

The alarm went off, signaling another door was open in the secured area. Everyone in the visitor's room sat silently as we waited for the inmates to come through a doorway, which had two officers standing on either side. Amy squeezed my hand a little tighter, and we locked eyes for a couple seconds. I gave her a look as to say, "Everything is going to be OK," but I honestly didn't know if everything would be OK. I didn't know if my mother might have forewarned my father that his youngest son was bringing his white girlfriend to see him. I didn't know if my father would start screaming and cursing at me for bringing her in a fit of rage. I didn't know if he would even acknowledge me after seeing what I was doing. Would he tell me, his youngest son, that he disapproves of the decision I was pursuing? Which was to possibly marry a white woman. Would he simply laugh at us because of the audacity I am showing right now? Would he be the butt of his fellow inmates' jokes after we left? He had been in prison for over twenty years, and as far as I know, he has never even shaken a white person's hand. *There is no need for doubts at this point*, I thought to myself. *This is my girl, love it or hate it, but it is what it is.*

The first inmate came through the doorway, and they were all smiles as they spotted their families. They continued to walk into the room in a straight line as if they were in a first-grade class. All with nice haircuts, newer sneaks, and shiny white DOC jumpsuits. Though their uniforms were loosely fitted, you can still see that they were in great shape. Their trap muscles and forearms were visible in their short-sleeved shirts.

Halfway through the line, I spotted one light-skinned guy towards the end of the line. He took three steps into the room and looked from left to right, trying to locate a familiar face. He made eye contact with me, but his eyes continue to pan past me.

“There he is,” I said as I stood up to get his attention.

“Where?”

I yelled, "Yooooo!" and waved at him to come to us. His eyes locked on me, then shot for a moment at Amy. He pointed at me with his index finger with a confused look on his face. "Doodles?" He said it in this low tone as if he was not sure. *He didn't know it* to be me.

Because we hadn't seen each other for many years.

"Yeah, it's me!"

He rushed over. We embraced. He gave me a bear hug with his left arm under my right arm, and his right arm over the top of my left arm and the four-foot wall separating us. I bearhugged him back. We held onto each other for probably 45 seconds and whispered to each other.

"I love you, boy!"

"I love you too, dad!"

"I miss you, man."

“I miss you too, dad!”

“Damn, thanks for coming to see me.”

“I feel bad I haven’t been down here to see you.”

“It’s aight. It’s aight. You’re here now.”

Tears built up in my eyes, and we released each other.

"Who's this?" he said with his hands on my arm. He could tell how big my muscles had gotten since the last time he'd seen me. As a scrawny teenager.

"Oh, this is my girlfriend, Amy."

He reached out to shake Amy's hand, but she embraced him with a hug.

"Aight, sit down," he said, pointing at the chairs. We talked for a while about how he was holding up inside the prison. I explained to him where I was working. At that time, I held employment at a middle school as a disciplinarian for at-risk students. This was my first conversation with my dad as an adult. I was attempting to pick his brain to understand how he thought. I said to him, "Sometimes these kids just can't see the future. One day, they are going to need the skills they are currently learning, but they just don’t seem to take them seriously. You got any advice for how to deal with them?”

"I was watching television the other night, and they were teaching the kids agriculture. How to plant and grow their own food. Those are skills they will need, too," he replied

"True, true."

In an abrupt change, I said, "So, Amy and I are thinking about getting married one day. What do you think?" For some reason, I can't do small talk for a long time. If there's something I need to say, I like to get around to saying it.

He responded with, “Why not? Do it.”

"I don't think her pop is going to go for it, though. You know, the color thing."

“Well, it’s going to be tough, but if you’re in love, it will work.”

That was probably one of my proudest moments of being Daniel’s son. Here this guy is, serving a life sentence in prison because of a white woman. A woman that was probably around the same age as Amy, who testified in court and said my dad kidnapped her. A white police detective claimed to have a photo of Daniel kidnapping her. A white state prosecutor put everything together and recommended two life sentences for kidnapping and eight dollars being taken away from the victim.

I walked out of that prison so proud of Daniel's strength. He wasn't letting the state take the heart pumping in his chest. They locked him up physically but failed to lock him up mentally. Daniel — after everything he'd been through — was freer mentally than most people in our society today. That takes a special kind of person. I looked at Amy as we pulled out of the complex, kissed her on the cheek, and asked, "What do you think? You've just met my pops."

"He's a nice guy. He was nothing like I thought he was going to be. It seems like he doesn't belong there."

"Yeah, I feel the same way, babe. I feel the same."

CHAPTER 18

ENGAGEMENT

Guess who's coming to dinner? ;)

I heard a comedian once say, "I got engaged on my birthday so that I would never forget my engagement date." I thought that concept was genius. Months before my birthday, March 6th, I had all my ducks in order. My mother and father didn't have any concern with me, asking Amy for her hand in marriage. It gave me such pride and joy that my parents had been through so much, in terms of race relations, yet they still didn't have a problem with me marrying Amy. On this particular day, I received a paycheck for coaching high school basketball, and along with saving up some coins, I was ready to buy a ring. That night, as I lay in bed, I watched a movie called Blood Diamond on DVD. My plan the next morning was to drive to Philadelphia, Pennsylvania, and purchase an engagement ring. The only problem was because the movie was so touching, I wanted a "conflict-free diamond." The film was based on the diamond trade in Africa, and how families have the option of either finding these diamonds that would be sold to Americans or suffer the consequences, up to and including death.

The following morning I headed I-95 North to spend my last dollar buying a ring for the woman of my dreams. I contacted her friend, Beth, days earlier to see what kind of ring Amy wanted. A three stones ring is what she told me. She sent a couple pictures that I had saved on my phone, so I was good to go. I went into about three stores, and everyone gave me the dog and pony show about how real and beautiful their diamond rings were. I was not a jewelry person, so I had no clue what any of the terminology meant.

I went to lunch around noon and said a small prayer while I was blessing my food.

"God, I have no clue what I'm doing, but I feel your spirit telling me this is the best thing to do, so can you please help me with finding a ring for Amy?"

After lunch, I walked into a jewelry store, and an older man was sitting behind the counter, helping a couple pick out a ring. He looked up.

"Sir, I'll be with you in a second."

"No problem."

I looked at the rings as if I knew what I was looking for. I pulled the phone out of my pocket to take one more look at the pictures as the gentlemen finished talking to the couple. I heard the couple say that they will be back tomorrow, and the salesman simply said, “I'll be here.”

I appreciated that coming from him. At the three stores I had been to in the morning, they would hound you and would even control the door, so you felt as though you were locked in. This gentleman didn't seem to be pushing anyone to do anything that they didn't want to do. He walked over to me and asked,

“Are you looking for anything specific?”

“Yeah, an engagement ring.”

“Do you know what kind?”

"'White gold and three-stoned,' I think is the name."

“Sure, we have about four of them. Let me show you.”

He showed me three rings and said he just sold the other one last night. Ring #2, a nice three-stone ring, would look perfect on her finger. We talked about a price that was more than what I wanted to pay for, but I really felt that this was it. This was the ring, but there was another issue. I looked at him and said,

“Where is this ring from?”

“I have no clue. Probably Africa.”

“Is it a non-conflict ring?” I then asked.

It was an awkward moment, and I have to admit, I felt silly

asking that question, but it was important to me. I had never visited Africa before, but I felt the need to make sure that this purchase did not fuel diamond trade, which, to this day, causes so much bloodshed in Africa. So many African men forced to mine for diamonds didn't sit well with me. Surely they had children and sons similar to myself, who are forced to grow up fatherless because of people like myself looking to please my wife while asking for her hand in marriage.

If my father had been present in my life, maybe I would be the catalyst in solving Africa's issues. Like Palestine and Israel, I could have brought the African tribal leaders together to find a solution that works for everyone. A solution that doesn't involve killing or forced labor. A plan that employs the local population and gives incentives to work for the mining companies. The local people could be taxed, along with the politicians at the same percentage, and use the tax revenue to build roads; invest in school; provide loans to local entrepreneurs looking to bring more jobs to the area, etc. If this were the case, I wouldn't be here conversing with this man about non-conflict diamonds.

He smiled and tapped the glass gently with the ring.

"Sir, if you want a non-conflict ring certificate, I, and any other ring store, can get you one. It would take me two seconds to go back and get you one, but that would be me not being truthful. Every diamond you see gets mixed in with the other diamonds before they get to the United States, so there is no way to really know."

"I appreciate your honesty," I said.

"That's why I still compete with all these big chains. People come to me when they are tired of getting lied to. I give them the truth, and they can take it or leave it. I won't make you do either."

Maybe it was a sales tactic of his, but it had me sold. I purchased the ring and had about $200 left in my bank account. On the way home, I stopped and got a fifth of my favorite drink, Hennessy. When I looked at myself in the mirror, I couldn't stop smiling. I was about to go and do something I have always dreamed about.

Amy had cooked me a meal around 5:00 PM, and my plan was to talk to my roommate E.J., then go to Amy's father's house to ask him for his blessing. As Ernest sat on his bed playing Madden Football, I told him of my plans to go talk to Amy's father. He paused the game and said,

"What if he says no?"

I sat back in the chair with the Hennessy bottle in my hand and thought to myself, "I didn't even think about that."

"He's not going to say no," I responded.

"Aight." Ernest shrugged his shoulders and cocked his head as to say, "Good luck with that."

As I poured our first celebratory drink of Hennessy, it hit me. This nervousness that I had in my stomach. It wasn't God preparing me for celebration; he was preparing me for heartbreak. Though it was my first time asking a woman to marry me, I knew it was going to go bad. I felt it deep down in my stomach. I was by no means a perfect man, but I worked hard to stay out of trouble. I was always respectful to my female friends' parents, and I have a plan for what life is going to look like when I get married. There were men in the past that have asked me to marry their daughter not because I was perfect, but because they knew I was a man of my word. If I said I was going to take care of someone for the rest of my life, they knew I would do it; but this…it felt different.

The stage was already set, so there was no turning back at this moment. After my second shot, I text Amy's brother's friend, Paul, and got the phone number to Amy's father's home. When I made the call, Amy's mom answered. I asked to speak to her husband, and seconds later, dad was on the phone.

"Hey Rashod, how's it going?"

"Good! Do you have a minute for me to come talk to you tonight?"

Dead silence. I could hear the hesitation in his voice when he started to speak again.

"Well, I'm just here helping clean up a bit. What time are you thinking?"

That was confirmation right there that it was not going to go the way I've always dreamt it would go. I have never been over to Amy's parent's home by myself, nor have I ever asked Amy's father to speak with him one on one in the almost two years we have been dating. Knowing what the outcome would be, I still decided to walk through the motions.

"I can be there in about an hour."

"OK. See you then."

While driving to his house, things just didn't feel right. My radio, which always played rap music, was on this country station. I quickly turned the radio off and pulled my phone out. I listened to an African who talked about how they do engagements, and I found it fascinating. What the man does is go to the bride's father to negotiate how much he is willing to pay to have the father's blessing. The father argues all the good things his daughter does and is, such as Cook, Clean, Healthy, Virgin, etc. The man asking to marry the daughter argues the negatives, such as Too Talkative, Too Needy, Bad With Money, and so on. It's meant to be a joke and a way of breaking the ice, as harsh as it seems. I figured I would use this strategy.

I arrived at his house, knocked on the door, and her mother came to let me in. If I could describe Amy's parent's house in one word, it would be "loud." Amy's immediate family consisted of nine children, so there was always a conversation going on somewhere inside the house...but not today. I walked in, and you could've heard a pin drop. A couple of her siblings were in the living room, which I passed to get to the family room in the back where her father was located. As he greeted me, I sat on a couch as he sat in a chair diagonally across from me.

"So, how's it going?" her father started with.

Me, not good at the "small talk," got straight down to it. I told him the joke from earlier about how the Africans negotiate on a price for the bride. I thought the joke was hilarious, but he didn't find it funny.

As we stared at each other with an awkward silence, I began,

"Look, I know that you know Amy and I have been dating for a while. In my culture, it is customary that I go to the father and ask for his blessing before marrying his daughter. What you think?"

"Well, Rashod, I don't have a problem with your race. I mean, Brett, my son, is dating a Black girl and I'm fine with that. This whole thing is new to me..." (I'm guessing "Thing" meant, INTERRACIAL RELATIONSHIPS) "...The first time I saw a Black person in person, I was in college. I came from a small town in Iowa where we just didn't have Black people that lived around us. Some might, you know, consider me a bigot. Maybe, I am a bigot. I don't know."

"Oooook," I responded.

At this moment, I didn't really understand what the hell he was talking about. I actually started daydreaming once he said, "I don't have a problem with your race."

You don't have a problem with my race? That's kind of all we are talking about right now, but … OK.

He started again

"When it comes to salvation, what's your belief?"

"What do you mean? I'm not sure I understand the question."

"I'll ask it this way. Do you believe the Lord Jesus Christ died for your sins?"

"I sure do. Do you believe he died for your sins?" I only asked that question because I became defensive. I felt like he was looking down on me by asking me that. As if his Jesus was somehow different from mine.

"Of course. So, you know you're going to heaven?"

"Well…I don't know for sure. If I turn to sin for the rest of my days on this earth and never repent, then I believe I won't be."

"Well, there is a problem. See, the Bible tells us that he died for everything we did in the past, present, and future."

I cut him off because I knew where we were headed. "So, you believe no matter what you do from here on out, you won't be held accountable?"

"No. That's what he died for."

"So, you can …"

He cut me off. "It doesn't matter."

"So, a person that calls on Jesus at a young age, but then turns into a child molester, and rapes women for the rest of his days on earth will go to heaven?"

"Sure he will," said Amy's dad.

"Well, I don't believe that. 'Faith without works is dead' [Bible reference], and I believe what the theology you describe does is take advantage of Christ, but if that's what you believe, then that's what you believe."

We were silent for a couple awkward seconds, and I was ready to walk out, but I didn't want to be rude. Now, at this point, I had been there for about an hour, maybe longer, and I still didn't have an answer. We started with race, moved to religion, and based on the way the conversation was taking place, I couldn't see what this had to do with me loving and cherishing someone for the rest of my life. One thing I noticed at that moment was that the butterflies in my stomach had gone away. Unfortunately, the shots I took with EJ had worn off.

"Well, in terms of giving you my blessing, I'll need some time to think about it. Maybe we can meet again and talk about it.

"Sure," I said, but it was the last thing I wanted to do. Even a blind man could clearly see that the answer was an astounding "NO." I continued hearing the front door open and close as he talked, but there was no chatter in the background, which was not normal. Anytime someone comes into the house, they announce that they are there, and everyone loudly greets them. I knew her siblings were talking about me in the other room. I'm sure her father told them about this before I even got there. It even crossed my mind that someone would sabotage my perfect proposal and tell her that I was soon going to ask her to marry me and encourage her to say NO. As we concluded that night, I walked out the door, defeated. Like a boxer who just lost the fight of his life. I tapped my pocket, which had the diamond ring I had bought with the last of my money, and yet I didn't know if I would ever use it.

Should I take the ring back, or should I fight for what I believe is rightfully mine?

As I patiently waited for a phone call from her father, I finally received one four days later. He asked to meet me at a Friendly's restaurant to get dessert and chat a little more. He said he realized he doesn't know me and would like to get to know me more before he makes a decision. At this point, I had been going over to weekly family dinners, birthday parties, and other functions to give everyone the chance to "get to know me," whatever that meant.

I know you can probably hear sort of an attitude in my tone of writing, and that's because it brings back so many emotions. I had never been in love, and here I was trying to do right, and for whatever reason, I was being rejected. I wished I had a father to show me how to handle situations like this, but I didn't. He was serving life and had no clue what his son was going through.

Is this what being a father is all about?

I was angry at my father, and I didn't even know the guy. I was angry at Amy's father, who said he didn't know me. I think a part of me wanted my hopefully future father-in-law to like me, but again, I was being rejected.

When we got to Friendly's, he had a small Bible with him. I knew this was going to become a sparring match of who can trip who up when it comes to salvation. As he threw out, "Works cannot get me in Heaven," I threw out, "Faith without works is dead." As he threw out Biblical characters that had been saved because of their faith, I threw out Judas, who had been handpicked by God and rejected later in life. We were going around and around in circles, and I still had no clue what this had to do with marrying his daughter, so I said,

"Look, religion was argued before you and I got here, and it will be argued when we leave, so there is no need for us to go round and round in circles."

We finished our ice cream, and at the conclusion, he offered me to meet with him and his pastor, which I reluctantly agreed to do. The following day, Amy came to me, upset. She wanted to know what was going on.

She said, "Everybody is acting funny, and it's upsetting me because I don't know what's going on." I explained to her what happened at her father's house and at Friendly's restaurant. She said she wanted to be there when I spoke with her father and pastor about the situation.

Six days later, we met with Amy's pastor on the second floor of their Church. Surprisingly, it turned out to be a pretty good meeting. Her father continued to throw out scripture, which her pastor agreed with, but he also understood the points from my side. After the meeting, he gave us hugs and told me that he would give me an answer. He then changed his mind and wanted to set up another time for us to meet again and go over things. We set a time for about five days later. Again, I was furious that we were ten days in, and I still didn't have an answer. The funny thing was that I wasn't pressed to have him send his blessing. I just felt like he was putting our relationship on hold, and that pissed me off more than anything. I had never had a father, and here I was with someone thinking that they can hold me up in life. *Not happening.* I thought to myself. *Not happening.*

Two days later, but twelve days after I asked for his blessing, I called his home to talk to him. Amy's mother answered, greeted me, and told her husband that I would like to speak to him. Because their phone was loud, I could hear him say, "What does he want now," in an agitated tone.

"Hello?"

"Hey, Mr. Weber, I hope all is well. Look just wanted to let you know I'm not going to be meeting with you and your pastor. I'm good to go."

"Why not? I haven't given you an answer either way yet?"

"It seems pretty clear that that answer is no to me. It's been twelve days, and now I'm going to make the decision on if I will move forward or not."

"OK, I'll let the Pastor know."

"Yeah, you do that."

Maybe that wasn't the most mature way of handling things, but I've never been good with playing the son role to anyone, and he wasn't my father.

My pops is serving life; I'm good to go.

Times after that didn't get any better. I stopped going to Sunday dinners and overall avoided the family as a whole once I heard that they were having meetings with her father and advocating for us not to get married. It was such an awkward phase of life for me. Mostly because at the time, I didn't feel like I had men to turn to. I talked to a couple of my boys about the situation, but I felt alone and lonely because I had no father to vent to.

On March 6th, my birthday it was pouring down raining outside. Amy called me over her house and cooked me ham, asparagus, and mac 'n' cheese. She also got me a present. After opening a small blue gift bag, I pulled out a pint of Hennessy. I've always hated for people to spend money on me for my birthday and Christmas because my mother would do it when we were young, and I knew she didn't have the money to do it, yet she did it anyway. But this meant so much to me on this day. When I looked in her eyes, I saw comfort, warmth, and understanding. I felt like I was in her world, the world was against me, and she didn't care. She put all that to the side and made sure I was happy on my birthday. I had made my decision.

After dinner, we took a ride to grab some drinks from the bar.

There was a running trail at the Newark, Delaware reservoir that we would go running at all the time. I told her to pull into the parking lot. She did as I asked, and we got out of the vehicle to walk to the top of the reservoir. The rain was coming down so hard we barely made it, but it was beautiful when we did. I asked her to pray with me. I prayed that God would always look out for us and help us make the right decisions. I then asked her, would she always be there for me? She answered yes, and we looked over the cliff and could see the bright lights of the whole Newark area. The area that took my father had never looked so beautiful. When she looked back at me, I wasn't there, I was on one knee. I looked up at her beautiful face as tears began to stream down like water from a fountain. I said,

"Will you, Amy Joyce Weber, marry me, please?"

She answered, "Yes, baby! Yes."

CHAPTER 19

DAY ONE OF PPD ACADEMY

Months later, while visiting my wife's friend Corrie, I received a call from the Philadelphia Police Department that I was being accepted into the upcoming academy class. I called my mother to let her know, and not surprisingly, she wasn't pleased. I understood the position I put my mother in, first by marrying a white woman and secondly becoming a police officer. On the first day of the Philadelphia Police Academy, I was as nervous as ever. I didn't know what to expect, and I didn't even know how I made it to this point. I sat in the Philadelphia police department academy parking lot and thought about my father. I asked myself the questions,

Do I really want to be a part of this organization? Is there another way to help my father other than this? With my father having the kind of background that he has, how did I even get here? Would there be any African American men or women that grew up in the inner-city in my class?

I hurriedly grabbed my belongings and headed to the building where I saw other recruits, dressed in tan khakis pants, tan long sleeve shirts, black tie, and a tan hat with the number 371 knitted on it. When I arrived at the door, a Puerto Rican male was dressed in a police uniform standing at attention. I walked up to him to ask a question:

"Excuse me, sir."

"Shut up and get in line," he said without even looking at me.

There was a line of recruits with their backs to a brick wall standing side by side. I counted 20 people when I walked up, but several recruits were still coming in after me. When the time hit 8am, which was the time we were told to report, I counted 53 recruits; eight were black males. They had us get in and out of formation for about an hour. They yelled:

"Get in line. Now get back on the wall. Now get in line. Now get back on the wall."

It was all a mind game to see who could be broken in the first couple of minutes. After they finally stopped screaming at us, we stood in a row of five, evenly spread out with ten people in each row. About five Sergeants walked down each row, inspecting each recruit's uniform. They then yelled at each recruit individually to make sure their uniform was pressed and boots shined. They also checked the recruits' faces to make sure everyone shaved with a razor, not clippers. One of the recruits tested their knowledge and decided to shave with clippers and tell them he shaved with a razor. They made him shave it with a razor and no cream or soap.

After about four hours of this, we went into the classroom. They separated all the recruits into classes A and B. The class split right down the middle. Class A on the left and class B on the right. On each side, there were tables that could comfortably fit three or four recruits. I sat to the left about 5 tables from the front in class A. You could hear a mouse squeak; it was so quiet in that room. No one wanted to get pointed out, so it was best you just stayed in the background.

While we were patiently waiting, in came Officer Anderson. He was a 50-something-year-old officer dressed in his officer uniform, blue shirt, and black pants. No one moved, but the Puerto Rican Sergeant came in yelling because we were all still sitting down,

"What the hell is wrong with you? Get up! Anytime an Officer, Sergeant, Luitenant, Captain, or a stray fucking dog comes walking in, you need to get out of your seats and stand at attention! Do you understand?"

"Yes, sir!" we all yelled.

The officers in his 50's had a smirk on his face as he looked at us all standing at attention. He instructed us all to sit down. He then told us he had a 30-year background with Philadelphia Police as an officer and that he would be retiring in a couple months. He said he was going to go over a cultural diversity course.

"They probably have me doing this course because I'm getting ready to retire. Ha! So if you're offended, you won't be able to sue me."

This should be interesting!

We started off by defining what a stereotype was. Next, Officer Anderson wrote "Jewish" on the whiteboard located in the front of the class. Next, he asked if any of us recruits are Jewish. Two people raised their hands. He instructed that everyone can answer except for the Jewish recruits. He started with writing the word "cheap" on the board. Everyone reluctantly participated until we had about ten stereotypes on the board. Then he asked the Jewish recruits about each stereotype to try to dispel them.

In the back of the class, there was one dark-skinned Asian recruit named Rann. When officer Anderson transitioned to Asian recruits, Rann was the only voice. Some of the stereotypes I remember were good at math, horrible drivers, good at karate, they live with extended family. At the end, like the Jewish stereotypes, he asked Rann to speak up for his group. Officer Anderson asked,

"Rann, are all Asians good at math?"

"No."

"Rann, what were your grades in college?"

"A's, B's, and one C."

Officer Anderson sarcastically asks, "What grade did you get in Math?"

Rann starts smiling. "A."

We all giggle, which was the first time we've laughed all day.

"OK, Rann, how's your driving?"

"It's good."

"OK, OK. When was your last accident?"

Rann laughs again, "Last month, but it wasn't my fault."

We all laugh a little louder as Officer Anderson puts a "T" for True, next to "horrible drivers."

"OK, Rann, home stretch. You're killing me here."

"OK, this one is easy."

"OK, Rann, do Asians live with extended family?"

"Absolutely not."

"Who lived in your house, Rann?" Officer Anderson said very slowly.

"My mom, my brother, my sister…my grandmom..."

Rann paused as everyone stared at him, and Officer Anderson held the dry erase marker in the air wanting to write an "F" for False on the board.

Rann then says, "My uncle, and a couple of cousins!"

"Nooo, Rann! Nooo!" Officer Anderson screamed as the class broke out in laughter. Officer Anderson then said, "You know what? I'm never doing Asians again. You're a piece of work, you know that, Rann?"

Embarrassed, Rann just laughed and shook his head back and forth.

We then moved onto African American stereotypes, and you could feel the tension in the room. No one wanted to say anything negative. It all started with good stereotypes, then turned negative.

"They dress nice, they wear nice-smelling cologne, they are athletic." And then, "They are lazy, always late, and are violent."

At that point, all the black people in the class said, "Aight aight, I think we are good."

We went through and dispelled most of the stereotypes that go along with African Americans.

Officer Anderson then began speaking about interracial relationships, which I was especially interested in. He said, "I don't have a problem with interracial relationships. I could see my son bringing a black girl home one day, but when my daughter bought Andre home, I had a problem. I don't know why I had a problem, but I did. I think it was because it wasn't who I saw her marrying one day. I expected her to marry a preppy white guy, so it was a huge shock to me and brought things out of me. I didn't even know were there. I had prejudices in me that I didn't know about, and so do you. Every single one of you. No matter how you grew up or who your best friend is." All the black recruits laughed. He continued, "When a nerve is struck, like what happened to me with Andre, those prejudices will come to the forefront, and you will have to take a step back to check yourself, and if it's your partner being prejudiced, you might have to check him.

I sat back in my chair and felt the butterflies boiling in my stomach from the time I walked out of my car, leaving my body. I appreciated this officer's bravery at that point. He did an amazing job not offending the white and black recruits, but finding a middle ground for us. This was amid a rise in police officers controversially shooting unarmed African Americans. Some of these instances were occurring in Philadelphia.

Weeks later, I still had this class on my mind when I saw the officer walking through the gym as we were working out. I stopped him and told him how much I enjoyed the course he taught, but I only had one problem with it.

"What's that?" he asked.

"You didn't tell us how things ended with Andre."

"Eventually, they broke up, so I didn't have a chance to make amends with him."

"I went through something similar with my father-in-law."

"Really?"

"Yeah, that's why I was interested in the ending. Do you have any advice for me?"

"Sure, just understand that we come from a different era. Young people these days think that we are going to change overnight and that's just not realistic. Give him some time. He'll come around."

"Thanks for the advice!"

I had high hopes after speaking with that officer. Unfortunately, right behind him, other officers and sergeants who would teach would drill stereotypes back into the recruits' minds.

At the end of the first day, we were shown a video of a corner store in Puerto Rico being robbed. The officers came into the store and were shot and killed by one of the robbers. The sergeant's explanation was that the officers made the mistake of trusting that everyone in there was a good guy. It was a heart-wrenching video, hearing the officer beg for his life after taking a couple shots and falling to the ground. The robber put one more bullet in him, and he was silent. Everything about his synopsis of the video was good until the end. He said to never trust anyone on the streets, especially in today's climate. People are out there to kill you. My point is that the video was horrible, and there is a special place for the young men that killed the police officer, but 99.9%

of the people we encounter will not have their mentality. So, should we treat 99.9% of the people in the community as the 0.1%?

During the class discussions, it became evident that most of the white recruits in the room were not from Philadelphia, nor have they lived in impoverished neighborhoods, which are the type of neighborhoods we will be patrolling. The higher-ups in the department passed a regulation that all officers were required to live in Philadelphia city limits for five years, but most officers figured out a way around it. They spoke of getting a rental property and living somewhere else or moving to nice, all-white neighborhoods. Though I don't think it's smart to live in the area you patrol, I think it's important to live around a diverse group of people because that will hopefully dispel some of the stereotypes we all have; especially the white officers.

CHAPTER 20

THE BEGINNING OF MY PHILADELPHIA POLICE ACADEMY CHRONICLES

During my time training at the Philadelphia Police Academy, I built several relationships with other recruits. The black recruits from the inner-city had our own small clique — for lack of a better term. Groups separated by color often occur at places of employment, but it was especially noticeable with Philadelphia police because of the current climate between law enforcement and minority communities. During instructional breaks, after the videos we were shown, which usually consisted of a minority killing or harming a police officer, we would make eye contact with each other across the room, as to say, "Here we go again. The big black man strikes again."

Interestingly enough, the one black male instructor we had, from my vantage point, had the same mentality as the white instructors and maybe even worse. His mentality, along with the white instructors, was not trusting anyone you came in contact with because they were out to hurt you. Though no one ever said, "Don't trust black or Hispanic civilians you were going to come in contact with," the communities

we were assigned to were over 90% minority, so this statement was implied.

They introduced us within the first couple of days to police encounters. A police encounter is anytime you, as an officer, interact with a civilian. That could be by speech or gesture. For example, speech would be a police officer asking a civilian what their name is, and a gesture could be a police officer pulling a gun out on a civilian. The three types of encounters we were taught were: Mere Encounter, Terry Stop, and Arrest. All three of these can have different names depending on what agency the officer works for. These encounter practices and case laws were taught to us from the first day we arrived all the way to the last day. Though the encounters are necessary for protecting civilians' rights, we were taught how to take advantage of civilians and legally violate their rights.

The first encounter we were taught about was a Mere Encounter. A Mere Encounter is exactly the way it sounds, mere, subtle, and harmless. This encounter can be a police officer asking a civilian, with, say, green shorts standing on the street, where is a good place to eat pizza? These encounters usually don't involve any paperwork because they are not investigatory in nature. The most significant difference between this encounter, and the other two encounters I will explain later, is that the civilian doesn't have to talk, nor do they have to remain in that location. They are free to leave at any point. In other words, the reasonable officer doesn't believe any crime has been committed, but because officers don't trust anyone, the law can take advantage of civilians during this encounter due to the police officer legally not obligated to tell civilians what kind of encounter they are involved in. Most people see a badge and uniform and think, "I can't just walk away from the officer." Therefore, they will give officers information that they are not obligated to provide.

The second encounter we were taught was terry stops, also known as investigatory detention. The name comes from a Supreme Court decision called Terry vs. Ohio.

A short explanation of the case: A detective in Ohio stopped three individuals, one of whom was a male with the last name Terry. The officer believed that the three men were plotting to burglarize a jewelry store. After stopping the three individuals, the officer searched them and found a gun on Terry. Terry filed a petition with the courts, saying his rights were taken away for no reason. The courts, as usual, agreed with the officer's actions that there was enough reasonable evidence to stop and "pat down" the three individuals for weapons. Hence, all law enforcement individuals are required to study this case and use it to their advantage on a daily basis. How do they use it to their advantage, you might ask? In today's society, 99% of civilians have one thing in their pocket that an officer will use as grounds to see what's in your pocket, and that's a cell phone. The Terry case, I previously referenced-- was upheld because the detective felt a hard object in his pocket, which allowed the detective to see what it was. Same thing in today's practices. Officers will feel the pocket where the cell phone is and then be allowed to invade the individual's space and legally violate their rights.

"If it turns out they don't have anything, just say you thought it was a weapon, and it turned out to be a phone or wallet," is what we were all taught.

An officer must have reasonable suspicion to stop someone for investigatory detention. A simple definition for reasonable suspicion would be the facts and circumstances that would lead a *reasonable person*, not an officer, to believe that a crime was about to be committed and the person(s) in question *might* have been involved. For example, say a police officer is investigating the robbery of a pizza store. A woman living on the street of the theft tells the officer the guy in green shorts across the street robbed the store and has the money and gun in his pocket. With that information, you can now stop/detain the individual for investigatory detention based on the information you received from the neighbor about the incident and their description. Once you stop him, technically, he is not free to leave, like he was during the mere encounter, until you finish investigating if he is the one who robbed the store. Based on the neighbor's information, the individual *might* be involved, but you must be sure before taking away all of his freedoms. During these investigations, you can ask him his name, age, where he is coming from, and where he is going. He doesn't necessarily have to answer your questions, but if he decides not to, you can take him in custody to figure out his identity. After a certain amount of time, if you have not concluded that he was involved, you have to let him go. Before letting him go, make sure you have his information, so if you come across more evidence or information, you know where to find him.

The last term introduced to us was probable cause. A short definition of probable cause is the facts and circumstances that would lead a *reasonable person* to believe that a crime has been or is about to be committed, and the person in question *is* involved. For example, using the scenario from before, if the officer goes to the pizza store after it was robbed, reviews a videotape showing the picture of a male wearing green shorts. You now have probable cause to arrest the individual. You can now take away all of his rights regarding freedom because you *know* he was involved.

Let's re-examine. When the officer saw the person in green shorts but didn't have any evidence, he approached the person and asked him questions like officers would do with the average citizen. When the officer only had information from the neighbor, he stopped the individual for investigatory detention to see if the information he had was true or false. When the officer saw the video and had the neighbor point him out, he knew the information was true, and he was arrested. All these encounters tie into police making arrests every day.

In a class discussion, after going over several examples, I asked, "Well, who's the *reasonable person* we are referring to here?"

"It could be anyone," one of the lieutenants said, "That's why we have trials and a jury."

"Sure, that's understandable," I continued. "But in these examples, are we referring to the officer as the reasonable person?"

"You don't think officers are reasonable, recruit Coleman?"

"Sure, they are."

I let my question die there because I didn't want the "good old boys" looking at me funny. My point was that what one person looks at as suspicious, someone else can look at it as totally normal. For example, we analyzed the Travon Martin case extensively in classes at the academy. It was amazing to see that every single non-black recruit felt like Travon was killed because of his actions — and that he was walking in that neighborhood, with a dark hoodie, was grounds to be suspicious activity if nothing else.

During the breaks every 45 minutes, we would have a ten-minute break to stretch and clear our minds. The recruits would often go outside to get some fresh air and talk to other recruits they were becoming close to. About four Black recruits, and the Asian recruit Rann, got in a circle and began talking about Trayvon's case. All of us had the same conclusion, nothing was suspicious except for a Black man in a hoodie.

Though Trayvon Martin and several other incidents where black males were shot and killed were discussed, we often only watched videos where police officers were justified killing a suspect. They would constantly put our minds in this one-in-a-million-incident, where the person happens to have a gun. The overall message that I got from encounters was, if you happen to kill someone, don't worry about it because we will find a way to make sure you're justified. Whether it's the cell phone in his pocket you thought was a gun, his movement before you fired the gun, or the suspect criminal record was justification for shooting the "unarmed black man," which was usually the suspect.

I wondered how all this information could tie into my father's case; so for the first time in my life, at the age of 26-years-old, I typed his name in Google to read up on the case. With butterflies beginning to start in my stomach, the first thing I came across was that my father attempted to have statements that he made suppressed in a hearing. From everything I learned in the academy, when you go to a suppression hearing, you do not say that the charges against you are false. You are just arguing that the police illegally got evidence.

What? Did he admit to kidnapping someone? I thought in my head. *How could this be? My mother always told me he was an innocent man, but this is saying that he admitted to it, which means he's a guilty man.*

To say I was infuriated is an understatement. I walked to my bathroom, stood in front of the kitchen sink, bent down, and splashed some water on my face. I couldn't f****** believe it.

I thought to myself, *how could my mother lie to me? She never lies to me. Does she even know that this is inside his records?* I picked my head back up from the sink and looked myself in the eyes through the mirror.

He's guilty. Like all these cases, I'm reading about where guilty people try to get stuff suppressed before trial. They're essentially saying, "It's mine, but the police illegally obtained it," I contemplated.

I then went into the living room to get my cell phone and call my mom.

"Yo, mom, did you know he admitted to it?"

My mother, not knowing what I was talking about because I was so furious, forgot to give her background on what was going on.

She said, "What are you talking about? Who's guilty?"

"Daniel." I was so mad I didn't want to call him dad.

"Your dad didn't admit to that."

"Yes, he did. I'm reading it now. The language they are using I'm learning about in the academy, and it's saying he admitted to it and was trying to take it back."

"That's a lie, Rashod. They were playing mind games with your father and tricking him into saying he did it. He would never do anything like that."

We got off the phone a couple minutes later, and I sat on the couch, thinking about our conversation. Was I to believe that the police tricked Daniel into admitting to kidnapping, sexually assaulting, and robbing a white woman? I would soon find out that this wasn't out of the norm.

The next week we had a class geared towards the district attorney's office and their role in the criminal justice system. When officers and detectives gather all of their information, they pass it on to the district attorney who charges the suspect. Before the trials, there are many hearings, one of which is where the suspect will plead guilty or not guilty. If the suspect pleads not guilty, the district attorney has to gather all of the evidence and present it to a jury that will make a final decision. If the suspect pleads guilty, that means the suspect is admitting to the crime. The judge will set a sentencing date, and the person will be sentenced.

Two questions I had were, what if the person is innocent but thinks the jury will find them guilty? What if the person pleads not guilty, but the District Attorney doesn't believe they don't have enough evidence to convict them?

Both of these questions have one glaring fact about them. They both sway towards the District Attorney (i.e., the criminal justice system). If the District Attorney thinks I can get a conviction because the evidence points towards the suspect, then they can ask him to plead for less time, so they don't waste the State's time and resources or, they can take him to trial and get him more time in prison. For example, if he/she is driving a vehicle with a gun inside, a reasonable person would believe that it's the driver's gun. The District Attorney would say you can either take three to five years and get out in two years or take it to trial, lose, and sit for ten to twelve years. As an educated person reading this, you're saying to yourself, "I'm not serving jail time for something I didn't do." But what if you were not educated, didn't have any money, didn't have any support, and were given a court-appointed lawyer who told you to plead guilty?

For the second question, what if the District Attorney doesn't have enough evidence? You would think that the DA would throw the case away, but unfortunately, that's usually not the case. The DA can offer you whatever they want to offer you before the evidence and judges get involved. The suspect knows they didn't do it, but it's like playing cards. You don't know what kind of evidence they have against you. They will even entice you by telling you that you won't have to do any jail time, simply probation. Most innocent people will jump on that because it sounds like a good deal, saves them money for hiring a lawyer, and, most of all, it's guaranteed except the guessing of what the evidence is that the State has against you.

So why wouldn't the DA just drop the charges against you? Because if that happens, the DA is admitting that someone's rights were violated by being arrested by someone who was a *reasonable person*.

During my academy process, when each instructor would introduce themselves, they would have the same modus operandi. They boasted about how many years they have worked as police officers, followed by how many years they worked in the toughest neighborhoods inside of Philadelphia.

They would then say, "I'm not a teacher or instructor like some of these instructors you have in here." Meaning, we should listen to them (street cops) and not the instructors. The teachers were also cops but may not have worked the tough neighborhoods — advancing in law enforcement career through education, a process that was frowned upon by "real" street cops. Their overall theme was, "I have to teach you this stuff in the books because of stupid judges and politicians, but when you hit the street, forget about all this and learn out there. Things will be different out there." Those words stuck with me throughout the academy: "Things will be different out there." What did that mean?

The instructors who were not your "street cops" could be spotted a mile away. Their uniforms were always pressed, their boots were always shined, and they were always well-prepared to instruct us every day. The street cops would say, "While they were making sure their uniforms look good, I'm out on the street making arrests." These non-street cops taught us the law and understood it, up and down, forward and backward, inside and out. Any question we had, they could give a reference to the law and why things went one way or the other. Their central theme was to connect with good police officers when you hit the streets. "There will be many police officers who will tell you, 'Forget about what you learned in the academy and listen to me,' but I'm telling you that they will be the officer that will get you jammed up and in trouble.

How could officers that come from the same police department and have gone through the same academy come out with totally different views on the academy process? Some of the officers who were "street cops" would even brag about how many times they had been to Internal Affairs for interviews.

When an officer goes to Internal Affairs, that means they are being investigated for violating someone's rights. Usually, this involves using too much force on a person. For example, cursing, punching, slapping, or shooting could have information about an incident that may have happened.

I could feel in the academy that you were there to make a choice. Which kind of officer will you become? A "street cop" or a "paper pusher" as some called it. *Would I, Rashod Coleman, Daniel's third son, be able to keep my focus and help my father? What if I have to be a street cop, to gain the knowledge needed to help my father?* They were questions I would soon have to answer.

CHAPTER 21

LOOKING IN THE MIRROR

At-risk Youth

Towards the end of my time in the Academy, our sergeant explained that we would have an assembly with at-risk youth teenagers. We knew every class had to go through the training, but we weren't sure what it would entail. We couldn't wear our police uniform or Philadelphia

Police paraphernalia outside of the Academy walls, so this would be the first time that anyone from the public would see us as police officers.

A lieutenant who would often teach our classes spoke with us briefly about what to expect during the training.

"This agency has changed quickly within the last couple of years, and they are letting just about anyone come and speak with the recruits. They also have some badass kids coming and a guy that is a part of the Nation of Islam. Do you guys know about the Nation?"

I was very familiar with the Nation, but there was no way in hell I was going to raise my hand, though I know he was probably only referring to the black recruits.

Philadelphia was taking steps to build community trust through cultural diversity training during recruitment at the Police Academy. This was due to the increase in cell phone video footage and the willingness of certain news organizations to air that footage of officers using excessive force. This training was brought about by one of the deputy commissioners, who was responsible for the idea. I believe there were two reasons for this training:

1. To show the citizens of Philadelphia that upper management was attempting to mend relationships between its citizens and police officers.

2. To introduce the recruits, most of whom never lived in high poverty neighborhoods or interacted with poverty-stricken youth, to the personalities they would be dealing with once they left the academy. Ninety percent of the time, while working as a Philadelphia Police Officer, you are trying to solve problems between people who are victims of residing in a poverty-stricken area. This training would be open for both recruits and at-risk teens to hear from each other in a controlled environment.

Throughout history, Philadelphia has had a strained relationship with its citizens. Two cases in particular that highlight this tremulous relationship is the killing of officer Daniel Faulkner and MOVE members. Philadelphia Police Officer Daniel Faulkner was shot and killed on December 19, 1981. Arrested at the crime scene was a person named Mumia Abu-Jamal. Abu-Jamal was tried, convicted, and sentenced to life in prison. Since that day, civil rights groups have tried unsuccessfully to get Mr. Abu-Jamal released from prison on a claim that he was wrongfully convicted. The second case that defines the relationship between the Philadelphia PD and its citizens was their relationship with the MOVE movement. The MOVE movement is a Black liberation group founded by John Africa & Donald Glassey. After several run-ins between MOVE members and the police, a Philadelphia police helicopter dropped a bomb on a Philadelphia row home, occupied by MOVE members, killing seven people, including five children. The bomb also destroyed 45 homes in the area. In light of legendary events like this, there has been a need for PPD to bond with its citizens.

When I first heard about this training day, I was looking forward to it. Because of the many discussions we had as a class, it didn't take a rocket scientist to figure out that many of my peers didn't have much experience with at-risk teens. At one time, I was what you would call an "at-risk teen." Though I wasn't a drug dealer, I lived in a neighborhood where most people's income was below the poverty level. It was not out of the norm for one of my friends to get shot, arrested for selling drugs, or arrested for shooting someone. At the time, I thought that every neighborhood was the same as my neighborhood. It took people having patience and understanding of my background to get me out of that mentality, which I felt these teenagers also needed who were coming to see us.

Our Head Sergeant, who was a 25-year veteran on the force, sort of warned us that the teenagers coming to speak with us were not going to be the most well-behaved teens. She also said, "If one of them decides to mouth off at you, don't be afraid to go back at them. They need to learn respect, so don't let them disrespect you by any means." I could understand what she was saying, it was just upsetting that the tone set was not to learn from them, but to teach them something. To teach them, the at-risk youth, that their mentality about Police Officers and life, in general, was wrong. This message given to young recruits from veteran officers was not only counterproductive to the spirit of the training but confirmed the incorrect preconceived notion that a lot of my peers already had, which was that the teens were a bunch of criminals.

My first teaching job, before I entered law enforcement, was at an alternative middle school. I was hired to be a physical education instructor for students who were expelled from school for a plethora of reasons. Some of the reasons were drug charges, gun charges, fighting, stealing vehicles, etc. Every single student in this school was considered at-risk. Everything from a student pulled the fire alarm at his school because he didn't want to take a test, to a 3rd-grade student who stole his grandmother's vehicle and drove it across town. When I asked him how he drove the vehicle, because of his short stature, he told me, "Coleman, where there is a will, there's a way." These preteens and teenagers were rough to deal with, but they all had one thing in common: They loved coming to school. No matter how much they got in trouble and kicked out of class, which was daily, they came back the next day. After being frustrated about this dynamic, an older white teacher told me this was the only place a lot of these kids felt comfortable. They could eat, were protected, and no one really knew what they had been through before arriving at the school. After I learned this, I stopped sending them out of class. My relationship with the students started getting better, and they began to articulate not only some of the struggles they had but struggles other students had outside of school. It wasn't out of the norm for me to hear, "Student One's mother is a drunk, and she beats him every weekend after coming home drunk. That's why his clothes were never ironed because he dresses himself on Mondays. Having this information about certain students helped me to be more understanding of their behavior. I wouldn't excuse it, but my tolerance was definitely longer, and that's what these teens needed that were coming to see us for this training.

The day of the training started off with the Deputy Commissioner telling us recruits to keep an open mind about the teens coming to the Academy. He informed us that all of these students had terrible interactions with Police, and he was hoping that environments like this could help them get past those experiences. After speaking for a couple minutes, he turned it over to a young white female and a middle-aged African American man. They both told our recruit class about their prior education and work experience, which consisted of studying teenagers' brains. They showed us a power-point of a 26-year-old man's brain next to a 15-year-old teenager's mind. They explained not only the difference in the psychological immaturity of the 15-year-olds brain but also the lack of physical development in the part of the brain that deals with consequence. In other words, they explained, "When teenagers make decisions, the part of the brain that says I will get in a lot of trouble for making this decision has not yet been developed. We are not making an excuse for them or encouraging you not to do your job, it's just something you can have in the back of your mind when dealing with teenagers once you get out of the Academy."

We took a quick break, and while we were on break, the at-risk teens had arrived on campus. They came walking into the gym, and I saw myself in these teenagers. It was as though I was looking at myself in the mirror. As they walked in, we took our seats, and they sat behind our class. There was a line of recruits behind me, and behind them were the teenagers. As the coordinator of the training called everyone back to our seats, one of the recruits, I had become good friends with while at the Academy, sat directly behind me. As I went to sit down, one of the teens sat behind him wearing blue jeans, white Jordan sneakers, and a black hoodie. As he sat down, he pulled his hood over his head. When I went to sit down, I reached over to him and put my hand out to shake his hand. Out of the corner of my eye, I could see several white recruits looking at me to see what I was doing. Because of the speech before the event, I guess it was supposed to be an us vs. them, type of assembly. The teen looked at my hand, reached out, and shook it. I held his hand a little longer than expected and asked him,

"Do you mind taking off your hood homie?"

He didn't say anything to me, he just took it off and smiled. I asked him,

"Where you from?"

"North."

"Where in North?"

"I'm not from Philly."

"Lehigh Ave."

"Cool. My name is Rashod, big guy! Nice meeting you."

"You too."

As I went back to my seat, the teen made eye contact with the female next to him. The recruit I had become friends with said,

"That's your man's Coleman."

"Nah, just a young fella that needs some guidance," I said to him.

The assembly started, and I was impressed by how smooth and well thought out it went. The counselors for the youth did a great job of talking to the youth and recruits about each side's struggles. For example, the Travon Martin case came up, and the counselor educated everyone about wearing hoodies.

He started with the question, "Who in here wears hoodies when it's a little cold out?"

Everyone raised their hands. "So, if we all love to wear hoodies, at a certain time of the year, how is it that it happened to be suspicious when this young man had a hoodie on? Conversely, who considers themselves from the hood?"

Almost all African Americans raised their hands from the recruit side and from the teenager side.

He continued, "So if it's midnight and someone comes walking down the street with a black hoodie on their head, and you can't see their face, what actions are you going to take? You're from the hood, you're in the hood, yet almost all of us would either cross the street or get out of the way of that person."

It was a simple example and, in the same breath, such a good one. We all understood that having a hoodie isn't suspicious in itself, but there are certain times that it could be suspicious. They

took several statements or questions from anyone who had something to say.

The moderator designated several individuals to go up on the stage and have a discussion. Representatives from Philadelphia PD, at-risk teenagers, and at-risk teenager counselors all took their places on the stage. One of the police detectives spoke of growing up in Philadelphia and being beaten by Police Officers. He said he joined Philadelphia PD, later in life, to become part of the solution, not the problem. Other than helping my father, being a part of the solution was how I saw myself also. One of the teens chimed in and made an excellent point.

"You couldn't beat them, so you decided to join them."

Such a great analysis from a 16-year-old. Without even thinking about it, he struck a nerve in the whole room.

There was a lot of going back and forth after that point. The same 16-year-old spoke of a time he and his brother were violated by two police officers. He alleged that two white police officers pulled his pants down in front of his brother, revealing his genitals in the middle of the street. He said his brother began crying and was extremely scared. He promised his younger brother that he would never let his brother go through that experience again. The translation of that was, someone, either myself or a police officer, would die if an officer disrespects me like that again.

The moderator passed the mic around, and none of us recruits decided to say anything. Halfway through, I decided to raise my hand and make a statement. As they came around to me, I grabbed the mic and said,

"I'm a person that wears hoodies myself."

The moderator grabbed the mic back and said, "We all like to wear hoodies."

He gave me the mic back, and I said, "With the current climate we are in with Police and civilians, we are not talking about everyone. We are talking about African Americans in inner-city neighborhoods wearing hoodies around Police Officers. The problem is civilians don't understand that officers need to keep themselves safe. Officers forget that while attempting to stay safe, civilians have a right to wear whatever they want to wear, whenever they want to wear it. Both sides have a right to be in that place, yet both sides don't want to budge for the other side. And that's when both sides end up on the news."

"Give a handclap for this recruit. Great analysis."

The moderator then reversed roles and did some role-playing. They had the teens on stage act as officers and allowed the officers on stage to act as if they were teens sitting on a street corner. The script was for the teens, in the role of officers, who had to get the officers, acting as teens, off of the street corner. The teens walked up to the officers and politely asked them to move, at which time the officers acted like civilians screaming about civil rights violations and Black lives matter. Though it was a little unfair because the teens were not trained on the laws and had no idea what they could and could not do, it was the best exercise of the day because you could see that the teens appreciated how hard it was to be an officer on the streets of Philadelphia.

The training ended with the deputy commissioner giving some words of encouragement to both groups. He urged us not to let the conversing stop at the end of this training but to take this experience back to our family and friends. Once he finished his statements, I made my way over to him to voice my appreciation. As a recruit or even officers, it was abnormal for someone to speak to the department's higher-ups. Philadelphia was really big on the chain of command, but that was a formality that I have never grasped. I felt like if I wanted to say something good or bad, I should be able to voice it to that person. I walked up to the Deputy Commissioner, shook his hand, looked him in the eye, and expressed how important and impressed I was with the training. I told him that it was such a good thing, and I feel it's really going to help bridge the gap between communities and law enforcement. He looked back at me and said, "Some of these recruits don't have a clue what kind of environment that they are getting ready to be sent to and to be truthful, I don't think some of them care, but if I can just change one of their minds about our Philadelphia teens, I think the training is a success."

He then looked at me and said, "Make sure you don't get caught up in the negative side of being a cop. It can consume you before you know it, brother, so stay focused on your reason for taking this career."

After speaking with him, I caught back up with my class, and we went back to our classroom to discuss the assembly and take another course. The teacher of the course was an old school Lieutenant with about 30 years on the job. He was on his way to retirement, but he still had a good attitude towards the Agency.

"What did you guys think about the assembly?" He asked before we started the course.

One of the white recruits raised his hand and said,

"It was horrible. Those teens are bad as shit, and we are probably going to be locking them up one day. The detective on the stage tried to explain the law to them, and they just thought they knew it all."

Another white recruit raised his hand and said, "And the BS at the beginning about teenagers' brain development was just an excuse for these kids to commit crimes and us to feel sorry for them."

I was astonished, but not at all surprised. Judging by some of the comments they made before the assembly, I knew they wouldn't understand the overall point of the meeting which was to do your job, but understand if there's room for discretion then use it because you know he is not thinking like a grown man or woman.

I raised my hand and said, "I loved it. I thought it was the most productive thing we have done in the Academy. Those kids reminded me of myself when I was 15 years old. I thought I knew everything, and it took people to have patience with me, that got me where I'm at now. At the end of our shifts, we will all go back to our beautiful families in our beautiful neighborhood, but there is another world out there, and we are in a position to help them, and I think that's what we should do."

An African American female recruit raised her hand. She wasn't one to speak out on anything throughout our time in the Academy, but she said, "Those kids were not what I thought. They were actually good kids. Some of the Sergeants had us think they were going to be terrible."

The Lieutenant looked up and said, "OK, well, understand when you hit the streets, they are not your friends. You can have interactions and be lenient all you want, but they will take advantage of you." I took his advice with a grain of salt. I did feel like he was a reasonable lieutenant, but I also understood the experience as an at-risk teen. He also said, "That 16-year-old teenager, I guarantee you will run across him again." Overall, it was my best day at the Academy. At that point, I was proud to be a Philadelphia Police recruit that was willing to stick up for at-risk teens, which went against the popular thinking of a Philadelphia police officer.

CHAPTER 22

HOMECOMING

My phone rang, and I looked to see who it was. I saw my mother on the other end,

"Rashod, your father's coming home next month."

"Really?"

"Yes, I just got a call today."

I was on my way home when I received that news from my mother. She was so excited, and I could hear the joy in her voice. It's been 27 years since she has seen him in regular clothing. When he went to prison, my oldest brother was eight; my other brother was seven, and I was three. She was forced to fend for herself. She refused to accept any government assistance and never put my father on child support. Through all my mother had been through, she still has a spark of joy in her voice. A spark that even I never heard from her before.

Conversely, I didn't know how I felt about his release. I didn't feel happy or sad. One thing I was especially worried about was my mother's happiness and emotions. I wouldn't want to see anyone locked up that didn't need to be there, but I would be lying if I said I wasn't worried about my mother being hurt by this man. I call him this man, not out of disrespect, but even though his seed created me, I had no clue who he was. I had spoken to him on the phone, written some letters to him and even asked him for advice but I still didn't know him. What's his favorite color? What's his favorite food? What's his middle name? All these questions made me keep a distance from actually embracing the fact that my father was coming home.

On July 31, 2015, my father, Daniel Coleman, was released from prison. My daughter was one year old at the time, and I scheduled to take off work to meet him outside of prison for the first time at the age of 28. While thinking about my first child, whose birthday we had just celebrated five months earlier, I couldn't imagine not being able to hold that girl or not give her advice, change her diaper and do all the manly things I have dreamt about. If, as a father, I have these rights, how could I deprive my own father of the same rights? Hypocritical at its best. As I got out of the vehicle, I felt a warmth come over me. I knew it was a sign from God that this was a good thing.

As I entered my mother's home, I yelled, "Dad," and I could hear footsteps coming from the second floor. It was like tasting a meal that I have never tasted before. I have never called any man dad before. It wasn't that I didn't have father figures around, it was because I never felt like anyone's son. I always had the vision that a dad would do anything possible to keep his children safe. I never had the feeling that a man would protect me over anyone else. So finally, yelling "dad" was overwhelming and breathtaking to me.

As I heard him coming down the steps, I took my phone and turned it on video. I told my wife to tape our first interaction. He came down the steps in one piece. After being removed from the family for 27 years, he was back. He and I hugged and exchanged I love you's for a long time. It just felt so normal, and I felt so bad for thinking that this was not going to be a good thing with him being released. It was like I was hugging myself, and if I was hugging myself, why would I not want him with my mother. I felt horrible. Tears began to build up in my eyes because I had fallen for what the justice system tried to teach us: All people that are locked up are animals. This was so far from the truth. This was a nice, kind, intelligent FATHER I was hugging. It wasn't just any father; it was my father.

When we released each other, I grabbed my daughter and said,

"This is your Granddaughter, Luell."

"Oh man, how old is she? He said.

"She turned one a couple months ago. She looked just like you when she was born."

"She's beautiful."

On my ride back to Philadelphia, I knew what I had to do. I needed to meet with him one on one and figure out what really happened on February 21, 1987. There was no way this was the man I've read about in that online article. This guy, my father, kidnapped a woman at 4:00am in the morning? I have to hear this for myself.

CHAPTER 23

FIRST DAY ON "THE STREETS"

Throughout my time in the Academy, several "street cops" would talk about 22th District. Located in North Philadelphia, it was known to be one of the most violent districts in the city because of the number of homicides it racked up throughout the years.

On my first day in the 22nd District, I noticed more African American police officers than I thought it would be. The sergeant I reported to was a short, white guy with these cool reading glasses and pressed uniform named Sgt. Smith. Though he wasn't a loud or braggadocious sergeant, it was hard for me to understand why every officer that came in contact with him, had so much respect for him. His introduction to us on the first day was really impressive. He told us that he spent most of his career in south Philadelphia, but after he began locking up the children of the people he locked up earlier in his career, he felt it was time for a change. That change involved him making sergeant and transferring his career to North Philadelphia's 22nd District.

He spoke for a little while longer, and I was really impressed by that part. From what I observed on the first day, he seemed to understand that just locking people up doesn't solve the problem. My mindset going into law enforcement was that although some people in the community commit crimes that warrant arrest, just locking people up will not solve the overall problems in these communities. From his first speech, it was evident that he felt the same way, which was confirmation my thinking was not as unpopular as I had thought.

After Sergeant Smith was done speaking, he handed out paperwork and told us the training officers we would be riding with would be in to get us shortly. About 5 minutes later, an African American female, standing at around 5'10", with a stocky stature from her vest, came walking into the room and yelled, "Who you got riding with me? I'm ready!"

All the recruits looked at each other to say, "I hope it's not me because she seems mean as hell."

“Coleman!” Sergeant Smith said with a smile on his face.

"Great," I said under my breath as I got up and followed her out of the room.

“Do I need to get any paperwork?” I inquired with her while walking to her vehicle.

“Nah, you’re good. Just put your hat in the trunk and get in.”

I got into the passenger side. The seatbelt was already buckled like someone had been sitting on top of it rather than wearing it. Our last couple of days of the Academy, a couple of officers talked to us about making sure we wore our seat belts. They showed us videos of accidents with people not wearing seatbelts, they showed us statistics. At a certain point, they threatened that if something happened to us, and investigators found we were not wearing a seatbelt, our families might not be taken care of. A street cop followed up the next day and said, "I guarantee, after the first day, all of you guys don't wear a seatbelt." I thought about that as she started the vehicle.

I have to start off by doing the right thing.

I unbuckled the seatbelt and put it on the correct way. I could feel the fire coming from her direction before I looked over. When I finally looked at her, she stared at me with a confused look on her face. "Fucking Rookies." She said under her breath as we pulled off.

As she pulled out of the parking lot, she hit the button on her handheld police radio and said,

"2211, Show me in service 2 man today."

“2211, Received. Have a good shift.”

The first call we got was, *A person appearing to be overdosing on drugs fell out of a window*. As she answered the radio, she simultaneously turned on her lights and sirens while speeding through the skinny streets of Philadelphia, which can barely fit small vehicles. During the Academy, we also learned that it was the law for us to stop for stop signs and street lights while going to calls. My training officer ignored every single stop sign and street light we passed. She even rolled down the window to tell someone to "Get the hell out the street!" as we sped by. When we arrived on the scene, I remembered another rule of the Academy: Always wear your hat outside the vehicle. My trainer stopped in the middle of the street, got out, and began fast-walking to the incident.

"I have to get my hat really quick. Can you pop the trunk?"

"She looked back at me with a look of disgust, slowly walking back over to the trunk, sarcastically turned the key and opened it. Obviously, she wasn't happy, nor did she reach for her hat.

“You ready now? The person is going to be dead by the time we get there. If I missed an arrest, I'm going to be pissed,” she said while walking to the house.

When we got to the house, there were already officers inside the residents, a rooming home. Rooming homes are houses where people lease out each room separately (illegally, of course). There was an African American thin woman, probably in her 40's sitting on the ground with an ice bag on her ankle. The officer training me told me to stay at the bottom of the steps as she entered the house. When she came back down, we walked over to the woman sitting on the ground being tended to by paramedics that arrived shortly after.

“What happened to her?” I asked the officer I was riding with.

“She was high on PCP and walked out of a second-floor window.”

“And she only has a hurt ankle?”

“I'm surprised she has that. They usually walk away. That's a powerful drug.”

She then turned her attention to the lady on the ground.

“Where are the rest of the drugs?”

“What drugs?” Said the lady looking up at her from the ground.

“The drugs you took. Are they in your pocketbook that you're clutching like it ain't no tomorrow?”

“I don't have any drugs.”

"Look, if it's drugs in there, I'm going to lock you up, so tell me the truth."

"If it is drugs in here, they are not mine."

"Give me the damn pocketbook."

The lady on the ground handed her the pocketbook as my training officer put some gloves on. She opened the pocketbook and took out three small bottles containing alleged PCP inside. PCP is an illegal drug usually smoked, and a side effect of it is hallucination. She gave her the pocketbook back and waved at me to walk to the car with her.

Great! First day on the job and I'm going to learn how to make an arrest, or at least do paperwork on these drugs.

Before opening the door, she stopped by a street gutter, and she threw the drugs down the drain.

"I'm not going to keep opening that damn trunk so you can hold the hat," she said.

"Question for you?"

"Shoot rookie."

"Why didn't we process the drugs?"

"Because we come across drugs every day, on almost every job out here. The DA and detectives are swamped, so bringing three vols of PCP is not smart. The detectives, your sergeant, your lieutenant, your captain, and everyone else would be pissed if you took up precious time to process that. People get shot out here all the time, so if you're tied up with this, who's chasing the real criminals?"

"Got it."

I understood what she was saying. I just didn't think it was right to be throwing PCP in Philadelphia drainage. But what else were we going to do with it?

Next, she pulled over and made a phone call. I couldn't hear who was on the other end, but I did hear her say I'm on my way. We parked on the street with government housing, commonly known as the projects. I could tell from Wilmington, where I grew up, that there were plenty of drug dealers hanging outside. She walked straight through their group, not speaking to any of them or saying excuse me. She knocked on a door, and a female in her 20's answered the door. Also, inside the house was about a 10-years-old kid.

"How are you doing?" the officer asked the female who answered the door.

"Good."

She then asked, "And how's he doing?" While pointing at her son.

"He's doing OK."

"If you start acting up, I'm coming back, OK? Did he get the money back yet?"

"Half of it."

"I'm going to give you until the end of the week to get that money back, OK?"

"Yes, ma'am," the boy answered in a tender voice.

As we got back in the vehicle, she explained that he stole $600 from his mom because he didn't want the school kids to think he was poor. She said, "I had to make the mom give him a butt whipping. She didn't want to do it, but we haven't had a problem out of him since. If she keeps going the way she is going, trying to be his friend, then he is going to be one of those drug dealers we just walked past standing on the corner. Those guys on the corner are why this neighborhood is this way, and I want them to know because I'm Black doesn't mean I'm your friend." Amid her talking, a foot pursuit came over the radio, and she stopped talking, answered the radio, turned her lights and sirens on, and continued talking to me about how to be a cop in Philly. I can't remember what she said because I was focused on hearing what was going on on the radio. The radio continuously gave updates on where the suspect and officer were, and why the suspect was being chased.

This is an example of how the call would be heard over the radio. It would start with the officer huffing and puffing; while attempting to give out information and keep track of the suspect.

"2212 ... Foot Pursuit ... Black male, red shirt, blue jeans ... running southbound on 2300 Montgomery street."

Followed by this is a long beep over the radio alerting everyone to stop what they are doing and help catch this suspect if they are close by.

Next, the dispatcher goes over the radio, "All units a foot pursuit in progress Black male, red shirt, blue jeans, running down the 2300 Montgomery street."

Next, all the officers in the area will go over the radio to alert dispatchers they are headed to that location to help.

"2214."

"2219."

"2215."

"2212, what's your location now?"

"Male turned right. He's now north on 25th street."

BEEEEEP.

The dispatcher came in, "All units be advised, Black male suspect is now running northbound on Montgomery Street."

"2219, I have eyes on the suspect. He's reaching for his waist!"

Everyone holds their breath to hear what the next radio transmission will be. Will it be that the police officer shot a suspect, or that the suspect is shooting at police? Either way, every officer in the area was speeding through the streets of Philadelphia to help.

BEEEEEP.

BEEEEEP.

"All units be advised the suspect ran through an alley on Jackson Street and appears to be reaching for his waist. Use caution."

"2219, we have the suspect in custody in the back alley of 25th and Jackson Street."

"All units be advised, suspect is apprehended at 25th and Jackson. Does anyone have eyes on 2212?"

"2212, I'm on the scene with 2219. Can someone check under the vehicles at 25th and Montgomery? The suspect threw a brown paper bag underneath a vehicle."

"2218, I'm on the 2500 block. I'll take a look."

"2218, be advised I found a bag of narcotics in a brown paper bag under a red Honda Accord."

“2212, I copy that transmission. I thank everyone for the help.”

BEEEEEP.

"Narcotics found and suspect apprehended. All units can resume patrol. Great job!"

During this first night of "hitting the streets," we probably went to 15 different calls. Most turned out to be nothing, meaning no one got arrested, but a couple of officers made gun and drug arrests. I was impressed that the officer training me took time out of her day to check up on some previous jobs. Also, she took the time to show me how and why everything on the streets can't go by the books, as was done when I was in the Academy. I found myself fascinated by the intensity and bravery of the foot pursuits, and it wouldn't be long until I found myself involved in one.

CHAPTER 24

FOOT PURSUIT!

On my second night with an FTO (Field Training Officer), I was assigned to work with Chris. Chris was a regular officer but had recently been promoted to a unit called 5-Squad. While I'm not exactly sure where that name came from, I quickly learned that you get on units, such as 5-Squad, from having a lot of activity. The "activity" can be anything from parking tickets to gun arrests. Essentially, you have been recognized by your higher-ups as a "Go-getter," so they assign you to this unit to let you find activity rather than respond to calls. My FTO from the day before was assigned to 1-Squad, responsible for answering radio calls. 5-Squad answers the radio, but they only respond to potentially dangerous calls such as robberies, shootings, stabbings, carjacking, etc. Also assigned to Chris for the day was a recruiter from my class named Kobe.

As we walked out of the police district to get into Chris's police vehicle, my main goal was to learn from the day before. As Chris put his hat in the trunk Kobe and I did the same. As I opened the door to get into the front seat, I noticed the seat belt buckle was already connected, simulating that the officers who used the vehicle on the last shift did not wear their seatbelts as we were instructed in the Academy. I watched as FTO Chris and Kobe got into the car and neither buckled their seatbelts. I grabbed the buckle with my right hand as I leaned forward into the front passenger seat with both of my feet still on the ground and, within a split second, decided to sit on the seatbelt like everyone else in the vehicle. Maybe I should have stood up for myself and done what was right. I wish I could tell you I was the tough guy to go against popular thinking, but at the moment, I chose not to.

We answered about 10 calls that night with Chris. For the most part, I felt like he spoke to us about our backgrounds and what we planned on doing while working for Philadelphia. Kobe and I threw out things such as moving up in the ranks, SWAT team, bomb squad, but both of us had no clue what those units did because neither of us had a background in law enforcement. We were just throwing out things to make us look like we wanted to be there and do a good job.

"SWAT team!" He said with a smile on his face. "You must be ready to take a bullet." Kobe and I looked at each other with a confused look. "Oh, they didn't tell y'all that in the Academy? The only way you move to positions like that, in this department, is if you take a bullet — either that or you know someone very important that can make a phone call for you. If you get shot, and the Commissioner shows up to your bedside and asks you what position you want, you can get SWAT. Surely, I thought he was pulling our leg until I happened to run into some officers from the swat team working in my patrol area months later. When I inquired how both of them got to the swat-team, without hesitation, one said, "I knew somebody," and the other one said, "I got into a shooting, and my partner was killed."

While riding with Chris, once I heard he was in 5-Squad, I expected the night to be full of car stops and pedestrian stops, but instead, we were just moseying around the streets. Later I found out that the 5-squad in this district was under investigation by Internal Affairs; so, they had toned back a lot of their police practices of getting a lot of activity. The investigation started not only from a substantial amount of complaints from the public but also from one officer in particular. No one ever said the officer's name. They would simply say, as Chris had said, "You'll hear about him soon enough working around here."

How can one officer get a whole district in trouble? It's not like one person can lock up the whole district. I mean, he's only one person, right?

I would later find out that he didn't arrest the whole district, but maybe three fourths. When dealing with civilians, they would often inquire about a guy they called "Maniac." "Maniac" was a legend to some and a terror most. When there was a shooting in the district and police needed to show its muscle, "Maniac" would be assigned to that area. Right or wrong, the streets would clear out, and the trouble simmered down.

Conversely, his practices were questionable, to say the least. According to local drug dealers and police officers, "Maniac" had a goal of arresting at least four people during his eight-hour shift, which is outlandish. Not to put salt on the womb, but the legend even says that he would make his first three arrests the first six hours, take lunch and go back in service to make a DUI. (Driving Under the Influence), arrests right before his shift ended. He, allegedly, got that last arrest so he could clock overtime hours and get a bigger paycheck. I'm not saying all these allegations are true, but when officers and drug dealers have the same story, it's highly likely.

That night was a lowkey night, but we got to pick Chris's brain a lot. He taught us where some of the popular drug blocks were and where they often hide their drugs. As we headed back to the district to shut it down for the night, Chris took the long way because he wanted to show us where a certain project (government housing) building was. Riding by the building, a Black male, about 5'10", wearing a black shirt, walked in the opposite direction of where we were traveling. My eyes were focused on him because he wasn't looking at us. Throughout the whole shift, every time we drove passed someone, they would intensely stare in the vehicle to see what officers were inside the car, but not this guy. As soon as he passed our vehicle, a Black woman yelled, "He just robbed me, he has a knife, and my phone." Without hesitation, Kobe and I hopped out of the car and started pursuing the man who began running once she started yelling. The first couple steps I stumbled, but quickly caught my footing.

This guy is fast as hell. I played D1 football, and there is no way this guy is pulling away from us like this.

He made a left, and seconds later, we made a left only to see nothing. He had vanished in thin air. Suddenly, Kobe said, "There he is" and started running down an alleyway. Something told me to keep straight to cut him off on the other side of the alley. Running straight, I came to a 10-foot-tall black gate surrounding the project building. Sure enough, the runner jumped on the gate only to see me on the other side.

"Oh shit!" He said as he gave up and didn't even try to get over the gate. Kobe grabbed him, I jumped over the gate, and we placed him under arrest.

We took him back to the vehicle where the female was, and they began to argue with each other about the phone. Apparently, they are in a relationship but got into an argument when she didn't want to give him her phone. Out of rage, he pulled out a knife, put it to her neck, and threatened to cut her if she didn't give him the phone. Furthermore, after checking his name, he had two warrants.

"I can't believe you guys caught him. He always gets away when the cops chase him!" She said.

"You'll never forget your first foot pursuit. Great job, guys," Chris told us while giving us fist bumps.

He continued, "I don't want to bust up the celebration, but you have to learn to listen to the radio while chasing someone. I lost you guys for a minute and had no clue where you were. Also, be careful going around those corners blindly. If he has a gun, he has the drop on you and your reaction is always slower. But overall, hell of a job. One thing we can't teach recruits coming out of the Academy is not to hesitate. You guys processed it on the run, and that was awesome!"

That foot pursuit was so exciting. It reminded me of the intense moments I had while hanging on Third and Broom street with friends. I would have to attribute the "no hesitation" to that area. If you hesitated on 3rd and Broom, that could mean you getting robbed or even killed. When you see something run, don't ask questions. Chris was a good officer and really loved what he did, but what I liked most about him was that he was focused on making sure we were safe. He knew we were rookies and just looking to run around and make arrests. He was true about most of that, but I was there only to learn the system that had taken my father away. Soon, I would meet a mentor that would help me along the way to reaching my goals.

CHAPTER 25

DEATH / TEARS / GOD'S PROMISE

"Coleman and Bahamonde, 24W1." My sergeant announces at roll call.

The first time I heard those words, I used to cringe. The area of Kensington I was working had multiple overdoses a day. That's right, almost every day there is an overdose, and when there is an overdose, officers have to transport the bodies to the medical examiner's office. I've always had a very weak stomach, so I am not a fan of seeing dead bodies. I wish I could say the same for my partner Bahamonde. He loved to see dead bodies--like really bad ones. When we first started working together, he thought it was hilarious that I was this big tough football player who couldn't stand dead bodies.

After seeing so many of them, I started to get used to it. When I first hit the district and saw these white officers smiling and cracking jokes about the dead bodies, I thought they were so insensitive, but after being there for a couple months, I saw it as just a walk in the park. I can't even remember the number of people Baha and I have saved through using Narcan. Narcan is a drug that you put up the nose of an individual who is overdosing. We would often respond to the radio call of a person overdosing in the middle of the street. When we arrived, we could tell by the color of the individual if they still had a shot at living. Baha, my partner, would get the Narcan together and administer it while I joked with the small audience crowding around. The person overdosing would have a gray haze to their face as life was leaving them. After he hit them with a dose, I would rub their chest around in a circular motion for the medicine to reverse them. We would yell, "Hey!" which would wake them up out of the dilapidated state. They would wake up without a clue about what just happened. It was like clockwork after a while, and I felt myself not being as sensitive as when I first started when dealing with the family of someone whose loved one had been killed.

I realized that I had a problem when I got a call from my best friend Casime after work one day. He told me that our good friend, T-Doc, had been killed. Shot dead in broad daylight on the same block we celebrated our talent show win in the third grade. We all loved that block so much, and yet, Doc was the second person out of our original crew that block had taken. Unfortunately, the first person had been T-Doc's little brother, Dirt, who was also shot and killed. At the funeral, it was awesome to see a lot of my old fellas from Broom Street. Halfway through the service, I remember looking around and seeing everyone crying. I wanted to cry and shed tears for Doc, but because of work, I couldn't. This was my good friend, a person I grew up with, a person that I loved, yet I didn't have one tear for him. I knew that I had a problem. Police work was beginning to consume me and take over my life.

Months later, my wife was 9 months pregnant with my son. I already had my daughter, and I was ecstatic that I would finally have a son. I had dreams and had so many visions about what he would be like and how our relationship would be. I was going to name him Rashod Coleman after me. His nickname would be "RJ." I couldn't believe God kept his promise and answered my prayers of having a girl first and following it up with having a boy two years later.

My wife was 10 days late with him, so we went to the birth center to see if they could help us get labor. They whipped up a concoction and around two in the morning, the day after my daughter's birthday, my wife's water had broken. She was inside the birthing tub pushing, and I was close by with my camera waiting for my baby boy. There were two nurses, one was the main nurse, and the other was a mentee. My wife pushed and pushed while in the water, but he would not come out. They kept close track of the time because my son couldn't be in the water for too long without drowning. The mentee gave her the time, and she told my wife she had to move from the birthing tub to the bed with my son's head sticking out of her vagina. I stood on the sideline, stunned at what was taking place. The joy that I had coming in had left me, and I knew there was a problem. She continued pushing, but there was no progress. I peeked to see him, and I could see his eyes were closed and not screaming as I had envisioned. The nurse looked at the mentee and said, "Call 911."

We pushed for about two more minutes with the nurse elbow deep inside my wife, attempting to get my son out. All of a sudden, he popped out. There was still a problem because he was stuck for six minutes. No breathing and no pulse, he just laid there helpless and lifeless. The nurse began doing CPR as we waited for the medics and police to arrive. As the nurse did CPR, she looked at us and said, "Call his name. What's his name?"

"Rashod! R.J. Wake up, boy. Mommy and Daddy are here," we screamed,

The nurse continued to give CPR as we continued to call him.

I started to have envy for God at that point. I began to question him and his tactics as I called my own name.

I can't believe you would do this to my child. My only son that I prayed for, for years. You are really going to let him slip away. I can't believe you. First, you let my father get taken — now, my son. I'm not Job from the Bible. I will be the worst individual you've ever created. My boy doesn't deserve this, God. My family doesn't deserve this. We have been through too much already. Can't you see that?

I looked at my son and no longer saw his face. I saw the lifeless bodies of the people that I saw as a police officer. My son now had that hazy look that drug attics had as they began to fade away into another life form. But this time, I wasn't joking with the audience because I didn't know what was going to happen. There was no Narcan to wake him up. In a turn of events, while she continued CPR, he gave a jolt as if someone just yelled clear and shocked him. His left leg moved, and he began screaming. Everyone took a long deep breath, and the medics arrived to whisk him away.

I rode in the medics as we raced to the Christiana Hospital with RJ fighting for his life.

“How is he doing?” I yelled to the back of the medics who were working on him.

“This kid is a fighter man. He’s not giving up.”

We arrived at the ICU, where four nurses were waiting to take him. I followed them to the back, and one of the nurses said, "You can't come back here, sir. Wait for him in that room." I began screaming, telling them I can't leave him.

"My fucking father left me, and I will never leave this boy. Somebody will have to kill me first." I can only imagine what these nurses were thinking as all the trauma from my childhood started coming out of me. "One day old, and you expect me to leave my little man?"

One of the African American women at the front desk gave me a hug and escorted me to the waiting room. I felt like I let my son down at that point. I sat in the room and cried as I have never cried in my life. After three hours, a nurse came in and said I could see him. I ran in the room to what looked like an 18-year-old nursing student holding him. She handed him over, and I finally got to hold him and protect him.

"Sorry I left you, man, but I'll be right outside this door, OK? You're not by yourself, OK? As long as I'm breathing, I'll always be here for you. If you need anything, just come tell me, OK?"

All the nurses began laughing.

"Your mom and sister are waiting for you to get out of here, OK? I love you, man. I love you so much." I passed him back to the young nurse who looked like she was having the time of her life holding my son. If nothing else, I learned that day to cherish life as I did before becoming a cop. To the midwife Nicole, from the birth center on 8th street in Wilmington, Delaware, we love and thank you from the bottom of our hearts. And PS, RJ hasn't stopped screaming yet!

CHAPTER 26

SHOTS FIRED!

As my partner and I entered the operations room after our Friday night shift ,my sergeant asked us if we wanted to work overtime tomorrow morning. She said we would have to report to the district and retrieve a police wagon to help Philadelphia's warrant team as uniformed Officers. We both agreed to which she said, "It will be an easy day. You should be headed home by 7 AM."

The next morning, as we waited inside the police van for the warrant team to show up, my partner, who had worked with this unit before, said, "We are only back up for the warrant team. We aren't leads, so we don't need to talk to anyone. Just back them up." Moments later, about five unmarked units pulled up and gave us the paperwork for the addresses of the houses we needed to be hit that were located in our district. It was a quiet morning, and even the drug boys were not on the corners. My partner, who was familiar with the addresses, looked at the paperwork and headed towards the first address. As he read the paperwork, he said, "Oh, this is just a basic warrant for a juvenile." At that point, it was about 4:30 AM.

As we turned onto the small Philadelphia street, there was parking only on the left side of the street because the block was only big enough to fit two vehicles. As we made the right-hand turn, Baha, my partner, jumped onto the street curb with the vehicle to avoid hitting the vehicles on the left side of the police van. We turned our regular headlights off to be as inconspicuous as possible as we parked in the middle of the street five houses before the target house. All police use this technique of not parking in front of a house because it gives someone a direct line to shoot into the vehicle from inside the house if they are tipped off. Because it is all row homes, you have to go back to each corner, turn down the block and go through the alleyway in order to secure the back door. Because the other officers were not familiar with these types of homes, no one secured the property's rear. Sure enough, as we exited the vehicle and walked towards the house, we could hear dogs barking inside the house. A woman screamed out the window, "Don't come into the house because my dogs will bite you. Let me put them away."

Next, you could hear dogs barking coming from the rear of the home, which usually meant someone was running through the alley. About four Officers began running to the corner to try to cut him off, and I remember thinking, *this guy is running like this over a small warrant, in which he will probably be bailed out tomorrow morning*. The woman finally opened the door, and we all entered the house. My partner and I were the last to enter. Warrant officers sat the female homeowner, a Puerto Rican woman in her 40's who was naked, on the couch with her Puerto Rican boyfriend, in his 40's and her 16-year-old daughter. Three warrant unit Officers walked up the steps, two officers walked toward the kitchen to search the house for the suspect. The mother who was naked attempted to get up from the couch and walk up the stairs to which I told her to sit down. She said, "I need to put clothes on." So a warrant officer threw her a blanket to cover herself. During these operations, the worst thing you can do is have someone walking around in places that haven't been searched. My partner looked at me as if to say, "You're working too hard."

After about five minutes, there was a THUMP, as if someone had kicked the back door. I was at the front door and had a direct line of sight to the property's rear. On my right was my partner, at the bottom of some steps. On my left were other warrant officers standing next to three residents who were sitting. When the thump noise was heard, everyone's eyes turned toward the back door, but because it was dim lighting in the dining room and no light in the kitchen, we couldn't see the rear.

I moved to the left out of direct sight of the door just in case someone shot through the door it wouldn't hit me. I looked at my partner, who moved closer to the steps out of direct fire from the back door. "Rough, Rough," was the sound of a huge dog at the back door. Somehow, the door opened, and everyone's heart stopped thinking it was the suspect, but a huge, all-black pit bull with a white patch on his eye came galloping into the room barking as loud as possible. I unsnapped my holster and moved another step to the left, and out of the corner of my eye, I saw a homeowner and warrant unit officers jump onto the couch as the Pitbull came across the threshold from the dining room to the living room. The dog was scared, and I can't blame the dog because, at 4:30 AM, nine officers in the house yelling commands at the only people he knew. I looked over to my partner, as the dog advanced closer to me and only saw the back of him running up the stairs. We had talked about situations like this in our police vehicle together, and the plan was that if we were ever in the situation where someone had a knife or a weapon other than a gun, he would tase them, and if it didn't work and the threat was still imminent, I would shoot them.

When I saw him heading up the steps, I removed the weapon from my holster and aimed at the dog. My eyes panned to the female homeowner standing on the couch, just as frightened as we were. At that time, time slowed down, and a picture of me shooting this dog appeared in a vision. I heard my firearms instructors say, "Get on your sites and squeeze slowly. Double-tap, Coleman." I came back to reality with the dog staring at me barking, and then the dog spun around in a circle, confused about everyone screaming in the room. I attempted to retreat out of the door by walking backward, but I forgot that I moved a couple steps to my left when I heard the thump at the door. I got the dog's attention with my quick movement and bumping into whatever was behind me; I think a television stand. He looked at me, gave one more bark, and began to advance towards me.

All I could think as time slowed down — even more — was, *"I don't want to be on CNN as being that officer that shoots anything walking."* I had dreams of going through 30 years in law enforcement and never shooting my gun. I wanted to be the example of an officer who has gone through his career the right way and shows that there is no need for lethal weapons. At this point, I knew that I was dreaming in a Utopia, and things happen, and right now, something was going to happen. I love dogs. I've had one since my stepfather, Kenneth, bought home my first dog we named Katrime when I was only eight years old. She was my best friend for years until my mother told me she could no longer live with us. One of my saddest days was when Kenneth showed me her picture in the newspaper's pet adoption section. I still wonder what happened to that dog.

There is nothing I can do about this dog in front of me right now. I wish I could have given him commands to retreat and go back to the backyard. We were past that point, and it was time for me to do what I had to do. I closed my left eye, which I learned in firearms training, lined up the three sights on top of the gun, and pulled the trigger. I didn't hear the sound of the "Pop," which is usually so loud at the shooting range. I smelled the gun smoke going through my nostril as it continued to advance.

"Pop," I let go one more shot, and it hit him in the body. He gave out a loud squeal as he turned and ran out of the room.

“Why didn’t you grab your fucking dog?” I yelled to the female homeowner as she began screaming, “You killed my fucking dog.”

"Shit!" I yelled as my partner came walking back down the steps. He quickly got on his radio to inform dispatch of my discharge. I retreated out the home, stunned by what just happened, but what happened next surprised me even more.

CHAPTER 27

AFTERMATH OF THE SHOOTING

Within what felt like two minutes, a Sergeant showed up to the scene. You can always tell who the Sergeants are because they have white shirts compared to officers wearing blue shirts. On the streets, it's pretty typical for civilians who were not cooperative to tell you, "Let me talk to a white shirt." That was slang for "Call your Sergeant." When the tall linky sergeant stepped into the house, he had what looked like a small note pad in his hand. Because it was 4 something in the morning, I had no clue who this sergeant was because he worked on the night shift opposite me.

"Coleman, come with me," he said in a soft tone.

Once we got outside, he told me to remove my weapon magazine, which I did. He then gave me a full magazine clip for my weapon. I looked up the block and saw that police tape up, and local news stations were already on the scene. About to reload my weapon, a vehicle pulled up with tenant windows, two white men with suits on exiting out the car, and began walking towards my direction.

"I'm from the Philadelphia Officer-involved shooting team. Were you the officer who discharged his weapon?" One of the men asked.

"Yes," I responded. As one of the shooting team representatives began talking, I can remember thinking *how the hell did everyone get here so quickly. I'm in the heart of the ghetto, and I'm pretty sure these guys don't live around here, and yet, they showed up in less than ten minutes.*

"OK. Briefly, and I mean, briefly tell me what happened. Give me the least amount of information possible."

"A dog entered the room, barking at everyone. The animal advanced towards me, so I tried to back out the door and realized the door wasn't behind me, so I shot at it three times. I believe I struck him once.

"And you only shot three times?"

"I believe so."

He then looked at my sergeant and gave him a nod to take me away from the scene. We walked the long way to the Sergeants vehicle parked a block away because he said we needed to avoid the news cameras.

As we walked to his patrol car, we stopped at a corner where two police officers were posted behind yellow tape. There were no media at that location. One of the officers asked me what happened inside the house, and I began to explain it to him. As soon as I started, the sergeant ordered me to stop talking.

He said, "Don't tell anyone what happened."

I really couldn't understand what the big deal was about telling what happened. It was a justified shooting, and there was a room full of people that would back that conclusion. Now that I am a more seasoned officer and have extensively studied courtroom procedures along with being involved with them, I know that one thing a defense attorney tries not to do is put his client on the stand. He doesn't let his client testify because the jurors who don't know him are trying to gauge what kind of person he is. That's why defendants come to court in a suit, a nice haircut, no facial hair. It's to try to get into the jurors' minds that there is no way my client committed these crimes. If you have a witness saying that he spoke with the defendant and the defendant admitted it, it is harder for the person to represent you to shape you in a good light.

Similarly, the sergeant was attempting to do the same thing with me. Even though I knew I had done everything by the book and had no other option but to fire at the animal, the long term implications could still be adverse if someone in the room were to say that I didn't have to shoot the dog. If that were to happen, I could end up in court and have to face jurors who would have to decide whether I had ill intent. Furthermore, if I spoke with people about the case, they would be called as witnesses, and now my fate could be in their hands. To avoid having something like that, you will usually never hear from the Officer until the case finishes.

As the sergeant drove me to the Internal Affairs officer, he told me to call my wife and only tell her that I was involved in a shooting, I'm OK, and it will be about twelve hours before I get home. When I got to the Internal Affairs Office, a Detective was waiting at the door for us. He greeted me and asked me to remove my weapon inside the lobby of the building. Then, he escorted me back to a room where there was a television airing the local news and told me to take a seat. The sergeant left out for a brief moment and back in to speak with me. He told me I was not to talk or text anyone about what happened. He told me not to even speak with internal affairs. He turned the television on, which ironically began speaking about my shooting.

"A Philadelphia Police Officer shot a dog, as a homicide suspect fled out the back door in his underwear. Before the suspect exited out the backdoor, he let a pit-bull into the house."

"Oh Shi*, you're a famous man!" Sergeant jokingly said to me.

"Nah, I'm not trying to be famous because of something like this. I had dreams of doing this job for thirty years and never shooting my weapon. I would come back after retirement and advocate that officers don't need these weapons."

He looked at me with a confused look and said, "Good luck with that, Coleman!"

Three days later, I was assigned to window duty because I was under investigation for the shooting. Window duty means you take all the reports for civilians who personally come to the district to make a report. As several of my fellow officers walked into the administrative office, they noticed me in plain clothes and working the window. Hence, curiously they wanted to know why I wasn't in uniform. Some of them already knew and just made jokes.

"Hey Coleman, Paws up. Don't shoot," Was the joke going around the district in regards to my incident. My sergeant, who wasn't there that day and was a huge dog lover (she rescued five dogs), called me at home to check on me. She told me not to worry about it and that things would be OK.

She said, "Prepare to be the butt of everyone's jokes, but everything will work out fine because you always try to do the right thing." It was a short conversation between us, but it was what I needed at that moment. She was a hard nose Sergeant who didn't take any s*** from officers, and it was hard to tell if she likes you or not, but to hear that she recognized that I was always trying to do the right thing was good to hear.

My wife called me upset days later after a Facebook post of the dog appeared online.

There is no way that this is the dog I shot.

The dog had a nice haircut, was clean, the tail wagged back and forth, and was moving around on three legs. Unfortunately, the hollow point bullet was so powerful that it had knocked his leg off, which hurt my heart. My wife was upset about the comments underneath the short cute video.

"What Kind of person would shoot a nice dog like this?" "It takes a real man to shoot a dog hu? Disgusting police." "What a despicable officer," was just a few of the things said about me under the article."

"I don't see why people are saying all these mean things about you," she said.

I told her to stop reading that stuff and not worry about it, which she eventually did, but I'm sure it was a tough thing to do.

Days later, I received a call from a lawyer letting me know I had an appointment with Internal Affairs to explain to them for the first time what happened. There was a young brunet waiting for me in the lobby when I got to the internal affairs building. She introduced herself as being my lawyer but seemed very preoccupied with texting on her phone. Before we went into the interview room, she told me to explain everything that happened on the morning of the shooting. It took me about 10 minutes to do, and she continually texts during the whole time I was speaking. She then stopped texting and said.

"When you get in there, you will leave [this] out and [that] out and just tell them [this]." Though she didn't tell me not to be truthful, I began to think that I did something wrong that morning. She explained that it's not that I did anything wrong, you just never want to talk too much in these interviews with Internal Affairs. Their job is to find something wrong. Everyone, including the homeowner's story, matched that story, so give them the meat and leave the bones.

The interview started and concluded in about 5 minutes. Anytime I began to give them too much information, the lawyer would stop me. She also was looking at the notes that the internal Affairs officer was writing the entire time. At the conclusion, I asked her why it was so short.

She said, "Because it's their job to find out if you did something wrong. The only way that can happen is if you tell them."

I drove off astonished that I didn't get to tell the whole story about everything that happened, but who was I to question someone who was there to represent me? It made me think about other shootings that were in the news and how officers involved in the shootings interviews went. Was there a lawyer telling them what to say and what not to say? It probably was, but I guess that’s just the way things go in the justice system. If you have good representation, you have no reason to worry. If you have bad lawyers, as my father probably did, it could cost you your life everything.

CHAPTER 28

CHANGE OF MIND

I was sitting in the living room playing with my daughter when I received a phone call. When I grabbed my phone to look at the screen, I saw it was my father's number. When I answered, I could tell by the soft tone he was upset. He told me that he received a letter from his parole Officer saying that the state is going to put a GPS on his leg and he is no longer able to travel outside state lines. Furthermore, my father, Daniel, would have to pay a monthly fee for the monitor.

He said, "I know I said I didn't want to fight to be exonerated, but I do now. Can you help me?"

"Of course!"

"What do I need to do?"

"Well, everything starts with paperwork. The arresting officer has to explain why they locked you up."

"Where do I get my paperwork from?"

"I'll go on to the Newark Police Department website and fill out the form to request your police report, but you will have to go there to pick it up on Monday."

"OK, no problem."

"Is my mom around?"

"Yeah, she's right here. You want to talk to her?"

"No, step away from her for a second."

I didn't know how their relationship was going, and I've never discussed anything sexual around my mother, so I felt awkward asking my father personal questions. She heard me ask him that because he was on speaker, so she said,

"I'll step out of the room."

"OK, mom, I'll talk to you in a second. Dad, I have a question for you."

"What is it, Rashod?"

"I know we have talked about this once before, but I have to ask you again only because I will be sticking my neck out with your case. I understand things happen, and sometimes you find yourself in positions, but If you knew this woman and she is just lying on you, or any story like that, I need to know now."

"Rashod, I've never seen this woman before in my life."

"So, at the time they are alleging that you robbed her, you were not there?"

"Nope"

"OK, cool. I'll fill out the paperwork and email it to my mom in a minute. Call me when you guys get to the police station Monday."

"OK, will do."

I went onto the Newark Police Department website and filled out the Request For Police Report form online. On Monday morning at around 10:00 AM, my mother called to inform me that they went to the records secretary at Newark Police Department, but were told they had no record of arresting Daniel Coleman. They informed my mother and father it must have been a different police department. My father was upset and adamant that it was the Newark Police Department. I then looked back on the website and saw a phone number for the Alderman's court. I gave them the number to the Alderman's court, they called, and the court confirmed that it was, in fact, Newark Police Department and gave him the report number. My mother and father went back to the Newark Police Department. They provided the secretary with the information from the alderman's court, to which the Newark Police Officer said, "Oh, yeah, I see it now. I'll gather the paperwork and let you know how much it is."

Two days later, I received a phone call from Newark Police informing us that they found all the paperwork, but because there was a substantial amount, the cost would be around $70.00 to gather all the forms. I called my father on three-way, and he told the officer that we didn't mind paying the fee for the paperwork.

When we got off the phone, I couldn't help but wonder why there was so much paperwork. I know the crime of kidnapping, robbery, and sexual assault are serious, but at .50 cents a page this a little extensive. I called my father back,

"Dad, do you know why it's so much paperwork?"

"No, I don't."

"Whenever I arrest someone, it's only 5-10 pieces of paperwork max. This seems so extensive."

"Yeah, I'm not sure, but we will find out on Wednesday."

"Cool. Call me when you get it."

I was so eager to get the forms that I drove to Wilmington from my home in Maryland, which is about an hour and a half ride to get my hands on it. I wanted to have a clear head when viewing the paperwork for the first time, so I waited until I went back home to view them.

The first page was a pretty formal report, nothing remarkable. The facts of the case were as followed:

On February 21, 1987, at approximately 4:15 AM, she attempted to withdraw money from an automatic teller machine on Main Street in Newark, Delaware. While she was operating the teller machine, before completing her transaction, the victim was grabbed from behind by a man who said, "this is a stick-up" and "I want your money." After a brief struggle, during which the man pressed a "hard [...] blunt object" into her back, the victim was forced from the bank's front to a parking lot in back. The victim gave what money she had to the man.

According to the victim, the man then demanded that she perform fellatio. However, almost immediately, the man changed his mind and said that "he knew of a better place." He forced the victim to walk back to the front of the bank and ordered the victim to get into the driver's seat of her car by threatening to "blow [her] brains out" if she did not comply. The man positioned himself next to the victim in the front passenger seat. The man then directed the victim where to drive the car.

As they were riding in the car, the man told the victim that he intended to have her perform fellatio. He also rubbed the victim's thighs and forced her to rub his genital area. As she was driving, the victim noticed a pizza shop that appeared to be open. She accelerated the car in that direction and jumped the curb. She was able to get out of the car and ran screaming for help. Several people emerged from the shop. During the confusion, the assailant walked away.

The police were called, and arrived at the pizza shop shortly after that, at approximately 4:30 AM. According to the first investigating officer, Officer Corcoran, the victim described her assailant as a "Black male, 5' 11" to 6'2" wearing a ski cap, had a mustache, wearing a light-colored coat, dark pants, white tennis shoes and had medium-to-dark skin."

At approximately 5:25 AM, another officer, having received a description of the assailant from Officer Corcoran, stopped Coleman in the parking lot of a restaurant located approximately one-half of a mile from the pizza shop. According to police testimony, Coleman fit the general description of the assailant, except for the fact he had a goatee and a mustache and was not wearing a coat or a cap. Coleman was questioned briefly about his identity and destination. Coleman stated that he was coming from his girlfriend's home and that he was on his way to work. During this discussion, Officer Corcoran drove by with the victim. She was unable to identify Coleman as her assailant. Coleman was detained no further at that time.

Later that morning, the police viewed a videotape taken by a camera that had been installed by the bank near the automatic teller machine. Both police officers who had seen Coleman earlier that morning during his brief detention viewed the videotape and identified the assailant on the videotape as Coleman. Coleman was arrested, without a warrant, later that same morning at his place of employment.

I called my father after reading the first page,

"Hey, dad, what time did you leave your house that morning?"

“Around 5:15-5:20.”

“How far was your job away from your house?”

“About a 15-20-minute walk.”

"OK, what were you wearing?"

"A flannel shirt, tan pants, and Adidas sneakers."

“What color were your sneakers?”

“White & blue.”

"Because the victim said the suspect had white sneakers on. Were your sneakers majority blue or white?"

"White with the blue stripes."

Man, I thought to myself. "That's not good."

"OK, dad, did you have a coat on?"

"No."

"Why not?"

"My flannel was thick, and it wasn't too cold out. If I had worn a coat, it would have just been another thing for me to keep track of at work."

"Did you own a tan coat with a hood."

"I owned a tan coat, but it didn't have a hood."

"OK. Cool. I'll call you back if I have any more questions?"

"Cool."

I hear my mother in the background say,

"Let me talk to him really quick. Hey, Rashod, isn't that an illegal stop because the officer said they were stopping all black males?"

"Well, yea. To stop someone *solely* because they're Black is illegal, but that wasn't the case from what I've read. He was Black, about 6 feet, in the area at the time of the incident, making the stop legit. If I was the officer, I would have stopped him too. It's too many coincidental circumstances for me not to stop him. The one thing that's hard to get around is the white shoes?"

"Yeah, but "back in the day," everyone had those sneakers. It wasn't like now."

"I get your point, but I would have still stopped him. Let me keep reading, and I'll get back to you."

"OK, we love and thank you so much for helping us."

When I got off the phone, I took a deep breath before going onto the next page. In my opinion, the officer that stopped him had more than enough evidence for investigatory detention; to stop my father and question him. Merely walking around at 5:30 AM is not a crime, but if someone just got robbed around the corner, it might be. Wearing white sneakers while playing basketball not is suspicious, but if a victim alleges the suspect had white sneakers on, it may be suspicious. A Black male, about 6 feet, is not suspicious, but if a victim says the suspect was black and 6 feet, that might be suspicious. All these things by themselves are harmless and innocent, but when you put these things together, they are definitely suspicious. I wish I could have told my father some good news after reading the first page, but everything was legit, and the officer did a good job so far, but soon I would see a hiccup.

CHAPTER 29

2 DIFFERENT CRIMES

The second page looked like a report from a possible detective. He wrote about responding to the same case as explained on the previous page but said he received a call on the police radio about another crime. The other call was for any police officer to respond to a burglary at Main Street Towers, which was just two blocks from the incidents at the ATM.

Why are they referencing another crime in his police report? I thought to myself.

When the detective arrived at the senior living facility, he was directed to a first-floor apartment. Inside the apartment was a 79-year-old woman being consoled by her son. Upon entering the apartment, the officer saw blood on the bedsheets and clothing that the woman who occupied the apartment was wearing. After speaking with the woman, she stated that she woke up to a male straddled on top of her. As she tried to scream, the male repeatedly punched her in the face with a closed fist. The male then turned her over, pulled her undergarments down, and raped her from behind. At his conclusion of raping her, the male walked into her bathroom and washed himself off. When he walked out of the bathroom, she could see he was a tall black male with a tan coat on. The victim lay still as the man exited out of the bathroom through the window. When she knew he was gone, she quickly got out of the bed and locked the window then called her son.

I stopped reading to let that sink in before I continued. What a horrible, tragic thing for anyone to go through, let alone a 79-year-old woman. That had to have been a nightmare come true for that woman. That story made me think about my grandmother, who is currently in her 70's. The story made me clench my teeth just thinking about what I would do to someone if they ever, knock on wood, decided to do something like that to my grandmother. Again, I had so many questions. Was my father arrested for this crime? Was there something he was not telling me? If he was found guilty on these charges, how is it possible, he is not in jail right now?

I quickly grabbed the phone to call my father and see if he ever heard about this rape. He answered on the first ring,

"What's up, Rashod!"

“Hey, I didn’t get very far in the report, but I see that Newark P.D. is referencing a rape. Do you know anything about that?”

"Yeah, they talked to me about it in the interrogation room, but it just went away."

“What do you mean it went away?”

“They questioned me on the night I was arrested, but I never heard another thing about it.”

“Did they charge you with it that night?”

“I don’t know, but I think so.”

“What question did they ask you on that night?”

"Umm… They asked me if I liked having sex, I said, "Yeah, of course." They then asked me if I like having sex from the back, I thought it was a weird question, but I said, "Yes, I do." Then they asked something about me having sex with an old woman. I said, "Absolutely not."

"So, eventually, they locked you up for it?"

“Yes, I believe so.”

“What happened when you went to court? Did you hear about it?

“Nope, nothing.”

“Then why would they put this in your report?”

“I don’t know. The only thing I can think is that they thought it at the beginning then dropped it.”

"I can't see them just allowing you to walk free in a case like that. I'll give you a callback."

This case was hard to read about. This is such a disgusting crime by an individual who never deserves to see the light of day. But was it my father who committed this crime? I know he says he was never charged with it, and it's not online, but as a police officer, I know plenty of people get away with crimes that they have committed. While working in the 22nd District with a senior officer, we received a call for a shooting on a corner that I was assigned to while on the foot beat. A trick that most veteran Officers would use is not going to the immediate area of the shooting, but driving in a direction that he or she assumes the suspect would head. One of the individuals who allegedly committed the shooting was a black male, blue jeans, and a red shirt. While heading to the scene, we noticed two African American males in their 20's, walking down the street, about four blocks away from the shooting. We stopped them but ultimately determined that they were not a part of the crime. When we arrived at the scene, a Chinese store was able to capture the shooting on its security camera. We watched the shooting, which showed two black males. Suspect One was short, heavyset, redshirt and blue jeans & Suspect Two was tall, around six-foot, jean jacket coat with matching jeans. Both individuals approached the victim and a dialogue between the victim and the suspect insured. The suspect, I assume, was asking the victim for some sort of directions. I make this assumption because the victim turned his back on the two suspects and pointed up the street. Next, the tall suspect began walking side by side with the victim as the short suspect walked behind him. Moments later, while walking down the street in the same position, the short suspect looked behind him to see if any witnesses were insightful, then pulled out a black handgun and shot the suspect in the back of his head. In addition, while the victim was falling from the first shot, he put three more shots into his body as he fell to the ground; before the suspects ran away on foot.

Those suspects, who were never found, are still walking around the streets of Philadelphia. I can only imagine the havoc that he is continuing to cause in that city. Similarly, my father could have just got away with this crime. As much as I didn't want to accept that my father could have committed a crime like this, I had the experience of being a police officer. Some of the best advice I received from my first sergeant was that "Everyone on the street lies to you. Everyone! No matter how cool or smart you think you are, they will lie to you."

In another situation, while still on a foot beat assignment, my partner and I saw a vehicle with its hood raised. As we approached, it was three African American males looking under the hood. I went over to see if I could help them out, after all, our sole purpose on foot beat was to build relationships with the community. While speaking with them and attempting to help them diagnose the problem with their vehicle, we started a conversation about local Philadelphia rappers. Throughout the day, my partner and I made about eight pedestrian stops, so we were not pressed to get more stops on the books. While I was having a good conversation with two individuals, my partner walked away from the group as we would always do when we were running someone's name. I didn't think that was the case because these individuals were not committing a crime, which is what you would need to run someone's name. And after all, these guys seemed like good guys. One of them asked if he could go to the store, which was at the corner to grab something to drink. We allowed him to go. Seconds later, our dispatcher called us over the radio.

"24FB1, is that male secure?"

Puzzled, I looked at my partner and saw that he had someone's identification card in his hand. He looked towards the store that he just told one of the males he could walk to. The dispatcher called again,

"22FB1, is that male secure?"

"No," my partner answered.

"22FB1, secure that male."

My sergeant came over the radio, "24FB1, place the male in handcuffs now. He has a warrant."

We ran to the store he told the male he could go to and he wasn't there. We ran around the corner to see if we saw him, but we didn't. Once we got back to the district, our sergeant was irate. All three of the males lied to us about their names, dates of births, and addresses, and only the lord knows what else. It puzzled me because it was such an innocent conversation we were having, and yet they were all simply stringing us along. Embarrassed, I promised myself to never let this happen again. I couldn't believe that we got jucked like that. I was a street guy who grew up around street guys, but that taught me that I still had a lot to learn about police work.

Situations like this always made me question what my father was telling me. Upon questioning him from the beginning, he never told me anything about a 79-year-old getting raped that night. And during his interrogation, he spoke of the detectives asking about sex but didn't put everything together for me, which is what I needed.

"Coleman, people will lie to you all the time. Never believe the first things that people say," was a common theme from my sergeant and though it hurt me in my personal life, I would have advancements in police work because I didn't take anyone's word. In police work, it's hard to turn law enforcement on and off, and the same goes for believing what someone is telling you. When speaking to my wife, I would often think what I thought when questioning a suspect. She or he is not being truthful. I tried my hardest not to bring that mentality into my personal life, but with my father, I had to keep my police censors on. I was in the middle when it came to believing my father's account of what happened that night. I didn't want to believe that these type actions would be in my DNA, passed down from my father, but I knew that, unfortunately, people that I have dealt with while performing my police duty were not truthful. As I went back to the paperwork to continue reading, I thought to myself that *there has to be a reason he didn't get charged with the rape*. And it wouldn't take me long to figure out why.

CHAPTER 30

WITNESSES

As I continue to read the original police reports, which were written by pen and by an old school typewriter, I got to a section in the documents that referred to witnesses. Witnesses? If there were witnesses during the case, this is an open and shut case. If someone got on the stand and pointed my father out as being the one who kidnapped this woman, there is no hope. And if that's the case, I would have to go with law enforcement on this one.

I take out a small tablet and write down the 79-year-old woman raped. Next, I wrote down the witness and circled it. I called my father back and asked him about the witnesses.

“Hey, they had witnesses against you?”

“What do you mean they had witnesses?”

“I’m reading here where the detective says that he interviewed witnesses.”

“Witnesses? I don’t know anything about a Witness Doodle.”

I threw my hands in the air.

Dude, you were serving life in prison because of what they testified in court to while you were sitting 10 feet away.

"Dad, were you at the trial?"

“Yeah, why do you ask me that?”

"Because they would have testified against you. If the District

Attorney has someone that said they saw you that night with this woman, they are summoned to court, and they have to go."

The cell was on speakerphone, so my mother could hear the intensity in my voice. She yelled from the background, "No one testified!"

"What did she say," I asked my father.

My mother's voice came closer to the phone. "No one came to testify against your father."

"How is that possible? They have to come to court."

"Well, they didn't. The only people that testified was the woman who said she was kidnapped."

"Really?"

"Yup."

"Are you sure? We need to get the trial transcript."

"I'm positive."

"Let me read a little farther. I'll call you guys back."

I hung up the phone, slightly confused. Maybe my mother and father were confused about what happened back then. I mean, it was 30 years ago. I opened the police report back up, quickly looked through the witness part of the police report, and saw six witnesses that night. Six! At 4.30 AM, in Newark, DE, there were at least six people walking about as if it was 4:30 PM? Something just didn't seem right to me. As I began reading the witnesses' statements, I learned three witnesses were at the ATM at the time of the abduction. Apparently, when the suspect dragged the woman to the back of the bank and decided not to rape her but take her for a car ride to a better spot, three people stopped at the ATM to retrieve the money. All three individuals remember the woman and man coming out of the alley from behind the bank. Out of all three of the witnesses, none could pick Daniel out in a lineup. Ironically, the line up is not even referenced in their report. I also found it extremely disturbing that one of the witnesses stated that the male who the victim was walking with was a *white male* with long hair. The Officer intentionally noted in that interview that the witnesses stated she wasn't wearing her contacts. In the three witnesses at the Domino's pizza when the victim jumped the curb in an attempt to get away, one of the males pointed Daniel out at the suspect in a lineup. The others picked someone different.

You have to be kidding me, of course, they didn't call them in to testify. These two groups all saw different things. They may not be bad people, but they are not credible. In fact, with witnesses four and seven saying that it was someone totally different in the lineup. The question I have is who else was in the lineup. There is case law that has set the presidents for line ups because of how biased they can be. A reference from a book called "How To Get False Confession," the retired DC detectives say that getting someone to point you out in a lineup is pretty simple. Simply keep the person you want to be the suspect in several line ups. That way, the person looking at the picture mind will remember the suspect you want him or her to remember without telling her. I know, simply disgusting.

But that's not even the bombshell for me while reading the documents. The fact that witness #1, stated that he got a good look at the suspect and was white, with long hair. If nothing else, that testimony brings doubt into the equation. In these cases, you need beyond a reasonable doubt and with a witness willing to testify that it wasn't even a Black person and that the male had long hair is doubt in a nutshell. I felt butterflies in my stomach while reading this. It was evident that the prosecution hid these witnesses from testifying, and there is case law for that also.

I called my father back and talked to them about the witnesses that the detective had interviewed. My mother became furious when I read the statement from the gentlemen at the ATM that said it was a white man with long hair. She began weeping as she put the pieces together in her head.

"They took your dad for no reason. Why would they do that?"

As a police officer and an officer of the courts, I had no answer for her. I had never seen anything like this before. To hide a witness is just...I don't know. I don't have a word to describe how I feel right now, typing this. All I can say is that it hurts. It hurts bad. How can I, a person who loves law enforcement, advocate for the criminal justice system that did this to my family?

CHAPTER 31

BACKGROUND

After reviewing some of his documents a week after I read about the witnesses, I felt I needed to have a conversation with my father. A lot of times, in the courtroom, they will harp on your past arrest and convictions. I know that when we get this case reopened, they may pull his old record. When I went to visit him, years prior, I can remember him saying that he was locked up a couple times in the past. If I was going to spank this case like I knew we could, he would have to do something that was going to be tough. He would have to be truthful about his past convictions. I called him around 10:00 AM.

"Dad, tell me about your past arrests?"

"Well, the first time I was arrested, a friend of mine asked me to take some money from a guy at the bus stop. The guy was standing there, so we ran up to him, snatched the money out of his hand, and ran away. My friend got caught and told them I did it. The police came and locked me up. The last time I was arrested, I saw television in someone's car, so I opened the door and took it out. The police came to our house and arrested me a couple days later. That vehicle belonged to the woman who owned the store that the vehicle was parked in front of. She saw me out the window and called the police."

I could hear the shame in his voice as he spoke his truth. I could only respect it but still had to look at it as a law enforcement officer.

"How much money did you steal the first time you were

arrested?" I asked.

"$1.00."

"Man, the DA probably checked this and saw that it looks like your MO."

"MO?"

"Modus of Operandi. It's like a pattern. Most criminals have a pattern of doing the same thing to their victims. Like if a guy is a burglar, he may always go through the basement window. So, the detectives, when they catch him, will use that pattern to convict him."

"But I did those things eleven years before that."

"They don't care about that. That doesn't make you a rapist of a sexual predator as they have labeled you, though. It just doesn't look good. Just make sure that you stick to the truth about your past. If they find you are lying about something in your past, it could hurt us."

"Definitely. Thank you so much, son. I know I've never told you before, but I truly thank you for helping me. The only person who has ever really listened and believed me was your mom and my mom. I love you, son."

"Well, maybe that is the reason God took me on this law enforcement path because I definitely have never liked cops." As I laughed at the irony. I didn't tell him I love you back, because honestly, I had doubts about his story at this point. These petty crimes could have just built to something serious. Nah, that couldn't be it. I needed to keep reading. I needed something to get me back on my father's side, and I would get it soon.

That night I got home and let my wife know I needed some time to go over my father's case. I updated her on our conversation earlier, and she, too, said that it didn't look good. We both agreed that it was a big leap for someone to go from petty crimes of taking $1.00 from someone to kidnapping, robbing, and sexually assaulting someone.

As I read the next section of the report, the detective stated that the male who rapped the 79-year-old woman actually tried to break into the home next door. Apparently, the male attempted to open the window next door to the victim, but the window was locked. I thought to myself, *how would they know he tried to access the window next door?*

As I continued to read, I saw that the detective was able to retrieve fingerprints from the window next door. The detective collected fingerprints from the window next door and compared them to the prints they found in the victim's apartment.

Wait a minute, I thought to myself, as I took off my new red reading glasses and placed them on the small round table, I had all the other documents. I sat back in my seat to take in what I had just read.

*Holy s***!*

I quickly put my glasses back on and continue to read. The detective then stated that he took the fingerprints from both apartments and compared them to Daniel Coleman, my father's fingerprints.

My wife yelled out to the porch, “Babe dinner is ready!”

"OK. Give me a minute."

The detective report then said that they concluded that the fingerprints were not those of Daniel Coleman. Hurriedly, I scoured the documents to find the description both victims had shared. Black male, between 5'5" and 6", with a tan cat and a hood on it. The descriptions were exactly the same.

The description wasn’t exactly the same, but they still charged him with one of the crimes. I thought to myself. I called my father back.

"Well, I found out why they didn't charge you with the rape."

"Why?" he asked inquisitively.

"They got fingerprints from the apartment and the apartment next door. Apparently, the perpetrator tried to break into the house next door, but it was locked. They compared those fingerprints to yours, and it was negative."

“Really!”

“Yeah, I’m not done reading yet, but I’m headed to dinner before Amy blows a gasket.

“Haha.”

As I got up from the table, I turned the page and saw the words:

FEDERAL BUREAU OF INVESTIGATION

All I could think while walking away from the table was, *"The FBI...man, you have to be kidding me."*

CHAPTER 32

FOIA

During dinner, I could not focus on anything that was going on at the table. I was only thinking of those three letters FBI. My son was making a mess, and my daughter was crying because she wanted something different for dinner. I quickly gobbled down my food and excused myself from the table.

"Can you get the kids teeth brushed before you get back to work on the case?"

"Sure. RJ, let's go.

I gave those kids the quickest dental work they have ever had in their life. I'm so bad, I know. I quickly got back to the documents to see what else was in these records. Two days later, the detective's notes stated that he drove to Virginia to drop the DNA I needed to call my father back, but before I did, I pulled my notepad out again and wrote down fingerprints. I also wrote down DNA, but I put a question mark after it because I was unclear about what they were referring to, so I called my father

DNA can close your casket in a case. If you say you were not somewhere, as my father was claiming, and they found your fingerprints somewhere at the scene, the courts would obviously come to the conclusion that you were there. That doesn't say that someone has committed the crime, but it does say that one, you had the opportunity to commit the crime, and two, you were lying. The courts would essentially come to the conclusion that if you were lying about this, then you were lying somewhere else. My father has never told me anything about DNA, but if they do have his DNA, then he was a liar, and I was done with him. Detectives can plant things, but from what I was reading, the officer who took notes seemed like he was doing things by the book, which I was really appreciating.

"Hey pop, was there any DNA presented in your case?"

"No?"

"You sure?"

"I mean, not that I can remember."

"Doodles, there was no DNA. Why do you ask?" my mother asked from the background because the phone is on speaker, and she could hear our conversation.

"Well, this says that there was some DNA dropped off at the FBI headquarters."

"Really? My mother says. Whose DNA was it?"

"I'm not sure. I haven't read the whole thing yet."

"But couldn't they plant your father's DNA?"

"Of course they can, but my experience as a police officer tells me that's not the case. The initial officer is doing a good job documenting everything."

I hang up with my parents and continue to read the documents. The officer states that he transported the victim back to the ATM, where she was abducted, which was only 4 blocks away, to see if any evidence was left at the scene. They found ATM receipts the victim dropped during the altercation, which he put into evidence. Also, he vacuumed all the fibers from the vehicle floor and seat where the suspect was sitting. There were also several fingerprints — nine, to be exact — lifted from the vehicle and believed to be the suspects. The detective put them all in a plastic bag and stored them as evidence.

After questioning Daniel Coleman and receiving his "alleged confession," detectives removed his shoes and made him comb his pubic hairs into an envelope. Furthermore, they fingerprinted him and added all of this evidence to the package that would be sent to the FBI.

The next day at work, by pure luck, one of my legal instructors walked by me as I worked out in the gym. We greeted each other and had some small talk, most of which I cannot remember because I was trying to get an opening into how I could get results of a DNA test,

"Instructor Taylor, I have a legal question for you."

He loved talking law.

"Sure. What do you have, Coleman?"

"When we get a rape kit, that's sent to the FBI, right?"

"Yeah."

"If someone wanted to see the test results, is there a way to get them?"

"Sure. You simply submit an FOIA request."

"That's it?"

"Simple as that. A lot of people who are not inside of law enforcement or the media don't know that. A lot of times, it's your right."

After we finished our conversation, I got on my phone to research FOIA, I saw that it meant it stood for the Freedom of Information Act. It was basically information accessible to the public, but you have to request it because it's in the FBI's possession. I called my father and mother from work and gave them the news.

"The only bad thing about this," I told them, "it can take up to two years to get back."

That reality hit us three hard, but we needed to push on. "We needed to push forward. It's been 30 something years since they locked you up, what's a couple more months?"

***

Three weeks later, I received a call from a Virginia phone number. The female on the other end of the phone told me she was from the FOIA department of the FBI.

She said, "There are 90 pages in regards to the request you sent. That could take up to 2 years to get to you. If we broke them down in two sections, I could have the results within six months."

"Yeah, let's break it up."

"OK, maybe if you tell me what you are looking for, I can send that part."

"That sounds good. I would like anything that says that the DNA obtained on the night matched the DNA of Daniel Coleman."

"OK, I get to that as soon as possible."

I didn't know what that meant, but I had to live with it. The woman didn't give me a, "There was a match" or, "There was not a match." Nothing!

I called and updated my parents. I told my father that 90 pages seemed like a lot of evidence.

I asked him, "Are you sure you were not in the vehicle? Because if you were, those records are going to say that."

"No, I wasn't in no white woman's vehicle."

"Cool!" I knew he was tired of hearing me ask that question, but I had to be sure.

Four weeks later, the day before I left to go to Puerto Rico on vacation, I received a package from the FBI FOIA division. The package came in a yellow large manila folder. Inside there was a disc with my father's case number on it. I called my wife, and we hurriedly pulled out the laptop to see what was on here. We both looked at each other and took a deep breath as the laptop loaded up. I called my mother and let her know we got the results. Her and my father patiently waited on speakerphone as we clicked my computer and saw the disk tab that said FBI. We then clicked the tab, and 50 pages appeared. The pages stated there were DNA fibers taken from the victim's vehicle floor carpet, seat fabric, and the jacket the victim was wearing on the night in question. They also confirmed that they received 8 fingerprints and one palm print from the passenger side of the victim's car where the suspect was sitting. Also, the FOIA department compared the fibers DNA to the sneakers Daniel Coleman was wearing on the night of the crime; pubic hairs and hairs from his head; all of his clothing and fingerprints. The division found that *nothing* in the vehicle was a positive match to my father, Daniel Coleman.

We all had a big sigh of relief as my mother began screaming and praying. I could picture the tears in her eyes through the phone. I also read to them that the documents were sent to the Newark Police Department months before the trial, so they had the information stating that the DNA was not a match. My mother woke up my oldest brother, who was sleeping in his room and screamed, "Your father was innocent, and they knew it. They knew it, and yet they tore our family apart anyway."

"Now we simply need to get this information in the right hands.

I'll make some copies, and we also have another 40 pages; so, we can't jump out the window yet, but this is worth the celebration!"

I got off the phone and felt the butterflies leave my stomach like a hungry kid who just finished eating. I can't believe someone would do this to me at 3-years-old. All the struggles that I've had not having a father could have been avoided. That's not to say life would have been easy, or that he would have been a perfect father, but I'm sure he would have stepped up to the plate and done his best. It would have given me more of a chance to do the right thing at an early age.

On this day, I was proud of my father for the first time, but this would soon come to a screeching halt.

CHAPTER 33

CONFESSIONS

My father called about two weeks later right before dinner and said he needed to speak to me. I could hear the nervousness in his voice. Not because I had heard it before, but because he sounded the same way I would sound if there was something I needed to tell someone.

After dinner, I stepped outside and called him back. I could hear the phone was on speaker; so, I knew my mother was probably in the room though she was silent, he began...

"So, say this goes the way it's supposed to go. What am I supposed to say if I go in front of the same parole board I went in front of when I got out?"

The officer in my head was confused by his question and not really understanding what he was saying, my police censors popped back on. I could hear the hesitation in his voice and the going around in a circle that he was doing. He knew what my answer would be. It would be the same answer I've been telling him the whole time.

"You said you didn't do it, so simply tell them the truth."

He knew this, but he was taking me around on a goose chase for some reason. On the streets as a Philadelphia Police Officer, one of the older officers used to have a technique for this. He would always say, "OK, I heard what you just said, but what's the underlying problem? What did you do? What did they do? If I don't know the truth,

I can't help you. You called me, so I'm not here to lock you up."

He taught me that people inherently always leave out their fault in the situation, and you need to figure that out in order for the case to be resolved.

"Rarely, do people have a problem with someone else out of the blue. Rarely do people ask you a question that they know the answer to. The only reason they are doing that is they need time to stall and see what kind of mode you are in."

"I tell them, cut the shit. You called me to help, so let me help you," was always the officer's line.

This is the position I was in with my father. He wanted me to help him with something but wouldn't say what it was. I posed a question to him.

"What do you think you should say?"

If this dude says anything...but the truth I'm going to tell my mom is to ring his neck!

"You always say just tell the truth no matter how hard it is, but I told them I did it!"

"What?" I said enraged. "You told them you did it?"

There was an awkward silence. I could feel my mother sitting on the bed, just looking at him. I didn't say it to Daniel, but I knew that my mother had made him call me or at least had recommended it.

"I told the Parole board that I committed the crime."

"Why would you do something like that?"

"That was the only way I could get out of that place, Doodles. It's hell in there. I was in there all those years, I just said forget it. The lifers told me that the only way I would get out was to admit it even if I didn't do it."

"What year did you confess to it?"

An awkward silence for about 10 seconds.

"2015."

Right before I could say something...

"2013, 2011, 2009, 2007."

WTF?

I silently motioned my phone as if I was going to throw it on the roof. I'm sure my neighbors would've thought I was crazy if they'd been watching.

"Yo," I wasn't calling him dad right now, "You confessed to this crime five times?"

"Yeah, every time I went up for parole?"

"I mean, I guess I'll ask the obvious question, did you do it?"

"No, no, no. I did not commit that crime."

He said, "I didn't commit *that* crime," which sounded like he had something to do with it.

"Did you know the female?

"No."

"Did you see her at any point on that night?"

"No."

I take a sigh of relief.

"Why didn't you tell me about this before now?"

"It's just embarrassing, man."

"Dad." He's back to being my dad again because I could hear the embarrassment in his voice. "Regardless of how embarrassing something is, you have to be truthful to me. If you know I will get tripped up about something you have to tell me. I don't care if it makes you look guilty, we can work around it. If I don't know about it, it could break us at the end of the day."

"I know, and I'm sorry."

"Look, dad, I love you, man, but if you're lying to us about something, I would rather you come out with it and deal with it. If we get to the end of this and find that you were lying to us, I will probably be done with you."

I can't believe I'm talking to my father like this, but he needs to hear it.

"And I don't know if you understand the severity of what is happening right now, but my mother is all I have, and she's very protective over her kids so if it comes out you were lying to her sons after all this time she may cut you off also."

"That's it, man, that's all I was hiding."

"You sure?"

"Yea, that's it."

"So why didn't they release you after the first time you confessed in 2009?"

"They said I didn't know enough about the case."

“How could you know about it if you didn’t do it?”

“That’s what I was thinking.”

"OK, well look, from here on out when answering a question on why you confessed, just be truthful, say, "I was in there for so many years, and I just wanted to get out. All the lifers who have seen people come and go told me the only way I would get out was to confess even if I didn't do it."

"OK! And again, I am sorry. I know you're on my side, and it's just a new concept and hard to grasp."

I went in the house for about an hour then walked back outside to give my mom a call.

"Hey, son?" she answered in her not-so-perky voice.

“What do you think?”

"Well, honestly, we don't know what he's been through. I told him to be truthful with you, and we are here to help him, so I know he feels bad for not telling you sooner. I cannot imagine spending a day in jail, let alone almost 28 years."

“I feel you. You think he knows more about the case than he’s leading on?”

“No, I don’t. I think he gave you everything he has.”

"OK, love you, mom."

"Love you too, son. Thanks for all you're doing."

I hung up and sat down on a chair with the original documents. I began reading another report from a University of Delaware Police Officer and thought to myself if my father didn't commit this crime, then who did? Little did I know, the answer was right in front of me.

CHAPTER 34

GAME CHANGER

As I continued to read the report, I was convinced that there was a crime that occurred that night. The fact that two different women, who as far as I know, didn't know each other claimed to be attacked in the same vicinity couldn't be ironic. So, there was a suspect out there, and with all the police that were called in to help find the suspect, surely someone had to see something.

In the University of Delaware, a college in Newark, Delaware, police were called into to help with the early morning search. The lead officer in the search that night referred to a supplemental report written by officer Johnson. As I sat back in my chair on the front porch, listening to the birds chirping, I skimmed through the paperwork and eventually found his report. I quickly sat up once I began reading what he wrote. According to the other Officer Johnson, while my father Daniel Coleman was being stopped, Officer Smith observed a black male with a coat over his shoulders, walking behind Newark Police Department. He transmitted the observation to police dispatch and tried to keep an eye on the suspect. When other officers arrived, he attempted to go after the suspect on foot, but unfortunately, he got away. After searching where the suspect ran to, Officer Johnson was able to find the tan coat that the suspect he saw was wearing. After retrieving the coat, he noticed the coat was full of blood and had a hood attached.

I couldn't believe what I was reading. If you didn't understand, at the same time, my father was released and walking to his place of employment, blocks away in the opposite direction, there was another suspect who got away. Officer couldn't find him, but they did find the coat he had, which was not only covered in blood but was also confirmed to be the coat the suspect was wearing by the victims. I called my mother to ask if they heard anything about the coat.

"Yeah, we heard about that during the trial," my mother said.

"Well, do they know whose coat it was?"

"Well, obviously, it was the coat of the person that did the crime."

"Dad, did your lawyer take the coat in the courtroom?"

My mother quickly answered, "No, they didn't. I asked his lawyer why she wouldn't bring the coat to court, and she said because it would make the victim look bad."

"Look bad? He got two life sentences, who cares if she looked bad?"

"That's what I was saying, but they did put a different coat up there, which was your father's coat."

"My Dad's coat?"

"Yeah, somehow they got his coat."

"I'll call you back, let me see about this coat thing."

I dove back into the paperwork to see if I could find anything about another coat. I read where after my father was arrested, the head detectives went to his home to check out his alibi, which was his girlfriend. The detectives stated that his girlfriend did, in fact, confirm that he was at home in the morning and left at the same time he always leaves for work. She also said the morning of the crime, he did not wear a jacket at all. When the officers asked to search the home, she rejected them. The following day after threats to get a warrant, she agreed to hand over Daniel's tan coat. Upon retrieving the coat, the detective complained the coat had no hood or a place for the hood to be attached; so this wasn't the coat that the suspect wore on that morning. The following day they got a warrant to search the house, but nothing of relevance was found. Apparently, during the trial, the DA had Daniel's tan coat in position for the jurors to see it, knowing that this coat was not the coat in question.

"Railroaded" was a nice word for what I was reading. I couldn't believe how flimsy this case was looking. I needed to see the trial transcript because there was surely more to this story than what I was reading. You have six witnesses, another suspect who wasn't found, DNA that didn't match, an alibi that says he wasn't where they said he was, and a victim who initially said it wasn't him. This has to be an easy case for the defense, right? The following day we got a call from the courts that the trial transcripts were ready to be picked up. You won't believe what I read.

CHAPTER 35

RAILROADED

As I opened the court documents, I noticed that the trial was only two days. Both the opening arguments were compelling. The prosecutor argued that they had videotape, and the defense had to first explain what a "videotape" was because it was 1987. The prosecutor was fierce in his depiction of my father. They labeled him a cruel black man on the hunt for white female victims in the early morning of February, 1987. This argument was nothing new in American history, but it was always compelling to a majority white jury.

The defense painted a picture of a man who was just in the wrong place at the wrong time. Headed to work in the early morning, he just happened to be stopped and questioned by an officer eager to arrest someone. She also argued that the picture you will see, which was allegedly black and white; grainy, and didn't have the victim in it, could have been any black male.

Throughout the case, the only witness called on my father's behalf was his then-girlfriend. Her testimony wasn't the best, and my father's lawyer tried, but I could tell she was out of her league. As a police officer, I've had times when I knew everything about the case and yet and still was ripped apart by the defense attorney. I have 9 months of training, a college degree, and a paid prosecutor to make sure I look good on the stand, and still, it didn't come out the best. I can only imagine how she must have felt having a defense attorney, who had never tried a rape case, put her up on the stand against the state's best prosecutor. At times when she would get flustered with his questions, she would ask him to repeat himself. He would follow up with the snarky comment, "Are you hard of hearing?" As if she was a five-year-old kid. She testified that she was up with him when he left for work, but she had trouble giving an exact time. In closing, the prosecutor claimed she was a girlfriend, so she would say anything to get him off.

My father, Daniel, did what most defense attorneys advise their clients not to do. Testify! I thought his testimony was solid. He stated while being questioned by his lawyer, that the admission that detectives said he made was false. He said when the detectives interrogated him, they often yelled, screamed, pointed guns at him, threatened to hang him out back, and repeatedly called him a *nigger*. He said when things calmed down, they asked him about his sexual activities with his current girlfriend. When he answered them, they said they were talking about the victim and not his girlfriend. He claimed that he was never read his rights, nor was he offered a lawyer.

I could only imagine him, my father, or me, myself inside the room being questioned. They thought that they were just questioning a 27-year-old Black male, but they were actually questioning his whole family. They were altering my life during those eight hours, and I had no clue what was going on. During the cross-examination, the prosecutor pushed him to say that he had admitted to what detectives had claimed. My father held strong and stuck with what he told the defense. When the prosecutor frustrated him with too many questions, my father asked if the question could be repeated. The prosecutor shot off the same snarky comment, "Are you hard of hearing?" He also pointed out the fact that my father didn't have a coat on when stopped by police. The prosecutor's insinuation was that my father threw the jacket down somewhere prior to being stopped by police. My father's claim was that one, it was not that cold out and two, he worked in a warehouse and didn't want to keep track of it all day. I haven't been able to find out exactly what the weather was in the morning, but the next testimony gave me a glimpse.

The victim, a 22-year-old white woman, was employed at her father's sub shop in Newcastle, Delaware. She testified that after leaving a night club called The Underground, which was located one block off Main Street, she dropped her friend off in a neighborhood called Todd Estates. After dropping her friend off, she went back to Main Street to find an ATM to retrieve the money. During cross-examination, my father's lawyer pulled a pretty good move. The victim stated in the paperwork that she took the liner out of her coat the day before, and when pressed to why she took it out, she stated, "It wasn't that cold out." That statement was in direct contrast with what the DA, and detectives' narrative, which was they believed Daniel tossed the coat because it was too cold out not to be wearing a coat.

The victim gave a chilling account of what took place that night, which really captivated the audience listening. Several times she asked the prosecutor to repeat himself, and not once did he ask her if she was hard of hearing. During her cross-examination by the defense, she was asked why she didn't identify Mr. Coleman when she was transported to the McDonald's, where Mr. Coleman was being questioned by officers. She said it was dark, and the officers never shined the light on him for her to see. Also, she stated she was too far away. This was all new evidence to the defense. On the night of the crime, she claimed that the guy that kidnapped her had a coat on, and his facial hair was different. She claimed that the kidnapper had a light goatee, but on the night of the crime, my father had a full beard/tsuni, as you will see Muslim men wearing. This testimony contradicted the officer's testimony, who transported her to the scene. He said that she was about 10-20 feet away from Coleman and shined the police lights on him so that she could get a good look at him. Her testimony concluded with the victim saying, "I am 100% sure that Daniel Coleman, my father, was her kidnapper and that his facial hair was different, but I know that to be him."

Different? I thought to myself. *Why would his facial hair be different*?

I immediately called my father after reading that. "Dad, what did your hair look like on the night of the crime?"

"I had a full Muslim beard."

"Listen to me closely. What was your facial hair at trial?"

"I cut it off. My lawyer wanted me to look presentable."

Again, I gave the motion as if I was going to throw my phone on the roof of my house. If you did not commit a crime and there is a question about how you look, why would you advise your client to cut your hair? The only thing that does is make you look like a suspect.

"That's crazy!" I said. "That's like court 101. Don't come into the courtroom looking like the suspect."

"Man, I didn't know. I was just doing what the person we were paying told us to do."

"Yeah, I can see. Anything else you can remember from the interrogation?"

"No, I think I told you everything. After they told me I was going to jail, they put a jumpsuit on me, made me put the hood on, and took the picture. That's it."

"Hold on, wait! What? They had you do what?"

"Put a jumpsuit on."

I quickly cut him off. "No, you said something about a hood. Putting a hood on?"

"Oh yeah, they got a jail jumpsuit and told me to put a hood on then took the picture."

"Listen to my question clearly, dad. What color was that fucking hood?" It was my first time cursing in front of my father, but I pulled that curse word out to understand how vital the question I was asking him was him.

"It was white."

"Dad?" He was back in my good graces again, "You know what that means?"

"What?"

"The only hiccup I had in the case was that one-person Id'd you as the suspect in a lineup. Because it was 1987 and there were only black and white photos, your photo would have been a whitish or even tan color. That means you looked exactly like the suspect in the photo lineup."

"Yeah, you're right. I never thought about that."

"I'll give you a call tomorrow. I need to read through the rest of the court documents."

"Cool."

I dug back into the documents for what was probably the one thing that could not be contested: That blooded coat and DNA evidence. I checked the police report at the same time and saw that the officer had received the coat and sent it off to the FBI. Again, my father's DNA was not present on the coat, either.

Perfect, I thought.

I went through the testimony of his supervisor, who testified that he was truthful about the time he had to be to work every day. She also testified that he was recently paid, which meant he wasn't in a tight need for money. I went all the way through the case and not one mention of the bloody jacket found during the pursuit of a suspect who was being chased while my father was being questioned. After the testimonies, my father's lawyer asked the prosecutor where the witnesses from the Mc Donald's and the Dominos pizza were? In another snarky comment, the prosecutor said, "It's not my job to call your witnesses."

I was floored when I read this. Here was my father, my mother, my brother, and I fighting for our lives, and his lawyer didn't know that she had to call and subpoena her own witnesses. Lord help us!

The judge allowed her to call a police officer and question him about what happened that night. Up to this point, there had been no mention of the bloody jacket or the suspect. She first called the officer that transported the victim to the stand. She asked him about the radio transmission he heard during the time he was questioning my father. That transmission was the transmission of another officer tracking a Black male with the tan jacket everyone was looking for. Rather than allowing the officer to answer, the prosecutor objected to the question and used the hearsay argument. The hearsay argument is that one can't testify about what someone else heard or saw. It's a good argument and squashes that Officer's testimony, but isn't this case about finding out what the truth is?

The judge agreed with the prosecutor and shut down the defense attorney. Frustrated, she rested. The prosecutor then asked the Officer if it was Daniel Coleman's picture on the grainy black and white picture. My father's lawyer attempted to object but was overruled. The officer testified that it was Daniel Coleman in the video.

Next, my father's lawyer called officer Mark to the stand. She had not spoken with him prior to taking the stand and didn't know exactly what he would say to her questions. It wasn't that she needed to lie, but as the prosecutor had shown earlier if someone was not going to be in favor of your argument, there was no need to call them.

Officer Mark was the Officer who called into radio dispatch about the male he noticed behind the police station matching the suspect's description. The Officer confirmed that he did indeed hear through police radio that Coleman had been stopped, and it was about 10 minutes after that he saw the male matching the description. Because the Officer who stopped my father said that he had my father stopped for about 20 minutes, my father was still technically in custody when they saw the suspect with the bloody coat. He said he conducted a search and found the coat with the blood on it in the same location where he lost the suspect. My father's lawyer asked the Officer if the coat he found had a hood on it. At that point, the officer gave an answer that totally blew my mind. He said he could not recall if the coat had a hood on it. When pressed about why he didn't know if there was a hood on the coat, he said, "I have not had a chance to review my notes."

Again, I wanted to throw something, anything off a roof. I couldn't believe this. Anytime we, as officers, go to court, the first thing we do is check our notes and anything we wrote down pertaining to the case. I have had cases that were a year old, and I could read my notes and recall what happened. This was amazing that the most important thing he was supposed to know he conveniently could not recall.

The defense rested, and next, she called one of the detective Reynolds, who was involved in the search and the investigation. When the attorney asked him if he remembered the bloody coat that was found, on the morning in question, the prosecutor objected again, saying no one established that a coat was found. He followed up with telling the judge that the defense attorney was attempting to talk about some coat that someone had found somewhere, but we didn't know who or where. The prosecutor did an excellent job of putting the judge and the defense attorney back on their heels. He basically explained to the defense attorney how she needed to ask the questions, then objected to everything she tried to ask. The defense attorney attempted to enter the FBI evidence and the coat into evidence, but everything was objected by the prosecutor, and the judge allowed it. He basically put her in a room with one exit, then blocked the exit.

As my mother waited patiently for the verdict to come back, she was told by my father's lawyer that it wasn't going to come in any time soon. After lunch, while walking back to the courthouse, she saw several people crying in front of the courthouse. When she asked them what happened, they said, with tears flowing down their eyes, "Your husband was found guilty. Double life."

There is a part that I left out conveniently while reading the testimony about my childhood. I had always thought I was a fatherless son at the age of three, but unfortunately, that was not the case. While my father's girlfriend was testifying, his lawyer asked his girlfriend how long they had been together. She testified that they had been together for two years before him being arrested. So, they got together sometime in 1984, which means I was only one year old when my father left, two years before he was locked behind bars for 27 years. I realized my father left me before he was ever taken away even though we all hoped he would come back when he got his head right. But getting locked away in 1987 ensured the ruin of all our lives. As I look back at pictures of myself when I was a child and couldn't find one with my father and me, it hurts to this day.

CHAPTER 36

DEAD END

When reading about the female victims, in this case, the names had very unique spellings. The only picture in my head was of this old white woman lying on a bed crying with blood all over her nightgown from the incident. Her right eye swollen shut and deformed face from the beating. Who would be so devious and cruel to do something like this to this poor lady? I could only think about my grandma going through a horrible situation like this. My heart skipped beats thinking about the victim waking up to this man breathing on top of her. Ripping her clothes off as she screamed for help. Repeatedly punching her in her fragile face with his big fists. I wanted to get to the bottom of this, but if I was going to, I knew I had to take emotions out of it and put my investigation glasses on.

I went back to the Newark Police detectives' original rationale, one person committing both crimes. If one person committed both crimes and my father, based on DNA evidence, didn't commit the second crime, that should prove that he is innocent!

My first step was to find the victim's date of birth (DOB). We were able to retrieve my father's information this way, so I didn't think I should have a problem retrieving the victims. I registered for a free 14-day Ancestry.com membership to see if I could find her DOB. Typing in her first and last name, I got a hit with her full name, DOB, and place of birth, Philadelphia.

"Perfect," I thought to myself while exiting out of the browser.

The following day I called the Newark Police Department to inquire about any paperwork having to do with her case. The same gentleman answered, who helped us retrieve my father's information.

"Hello, I'm requesting any information having to do with a case from 1987."

"What's the name and DOB?" He asked.

I gave him the information. After a few minutes of being on hold, he came back on the line.

"What do you need the information for?"

"I'm writing a book about that night."

"One moment, please."

After sitting on hold for about 30 seconds, he returned.

"Unfortunately, sir, I can't give you any of her information."

"Why not?"

"You are not a part of the case; so, I can't give it to you."

After we got off of the phone, I called the alderman's court. The secretary explained to me that there was no record of her in her system. She also told me to fill out a Freedom of Information Act Request, and maybe the city's lawyers would release the information. The following day I filed an FOIA request online and waited for a response.

Two days later, I received an email from Alderman's court stating my request was denied. I called back to the courts to follow up on the denial. The secretary told me that the documents are sealed and because I was not a part of the case, I am not at liberty to receive them. After hanging up the phone, I called back to the Newark Police Department to see if someone else might pick up the phone and help me. To my surprise, an older woman picked up a different person than I was speaking to days prior. After briefly speaking to her about the case and the documents I was requesting, she put me on hold.

Twenty seconds later, she returned and said, "I'm a little swamped with paperwork now, but I have found her information in our system. I'll call you back in an hour to see what forms you want."

Three hours went by, and there was still no call from her. I checked my phone and called it on my wife's phone to make sure it was working correctly. This phone call could change everything for my father and our family. If I could find the name of the person arrested for the assault, I could match his fingerprints with the fingerprints in the vehicle, and we would be done with this case.

I could wait no longer, so I decided to call. The young man I spoke to answered the phone first, so I disguised my voice and asked for the female. When she explained, she apologized for not getting back with me but put me on hold to check. After returning, she asked,

"Do you have the defendant's name?"

"No, I only have the victim's name. I'm looking for the defendant's name."

"It looks like this case was taken over by the Federal Bureau of Investigations (FBI)!"

"Really?"

"Yes, but let me ask my co-worker. One minute please."

She returns in 10 seconds.

"Sir, are you related to the victim?"

"No."

"My co-worker has already spoken to you, sir. I can't give you any information."

When we got off the phone, I was puzzled by why her attitude had shifted after she spoke to her co-worker. I was disappointed that I didn't get any information but hopeful because she had given me a vital piece of information without knowing. She said this case had been taken over by the FBI. I knew from my police work that the crime had crossed state lines. Because I had already completed an FOIA request through the FBI. It wasn't going to be a problem doing another. Unfortunately, one month later, the FBI had denied that request.

I went back to the drawing board. I pulled back out the original documents and began to scan through them. Clear as day, something jumped out at me. When the police officer arrived on the scene for the rape, her son, was already there. The police report stated that after the suspect departed, the victim called her son, who then called the police.

Maybe her son knows if someone was ever charged with his mother's assault. I contemplated while lying on my back, staring up at the ceiling before bed. I then pulled my phone out and typed his name into google. Millions of people with her son's name came up, so I ordered another Ancestry.com membership in my wife's email so I could take advantage of it being free. I typed his name in and got a hit through Newspaper.com, requiring me to get a free subscription for 14 days. I signed up for the subscription and typed the victim's full name only to see if I could find some information. If she was alive, she would be over 100 years old, but it's worth a shot. I typed in her full name only to see it referencing that her son, my only witness to the crime scene, died in 1995 — another dead end.

***

I decided to type in her son's full name into newspaper.com, and I received about four hits, one of which was his obituary. Not only did it mention his mother — but it also mentioned his children living in a place called The Village, Florida.

Maybe he told his children about what happened, I thought.

I went to Facebook and typed in his name along with Florida, and a grandson of the rape victim popped up in a police uniform. After further research, I found that not only was his son was a police officer but also his father. Surely they would know about this investigation, right? I went to sleep that night with the son and grandson of the rape victim on my mind. I silently prayed to myself, "God send me a message on what to do next."

Two days later, I received a message from my wife's aunt, Elaine, Elaine was a tall white woman with glasses that gives the best hugs ever. Though she seemed to come from a Republican family, she was a Democrat. I think a lot of her views came from her work with adopted children, but I could be wrong. Elaine did some research for me regarding my family a year earlier. I was trying to research where my family came from, which was hard because they were slaves, and their records were either not documented or destroyed. Her email asked how my research was going with my family history and my father. I explained that I had some names, and it referenced a place called Village, Florida. She explained that Village, Florida, was about 15 minutes from where she lives.

“Give me the names and let me see what I can find.” She said.

I gave her all the names that I had, and the next day she emailed me back with a full profile of the grandson. I called a couple of the numbers on the profile, but they were all out of service. I emailed her back to let her know, and she simply said, "Send an Email."

I sent a generic email with the subject stating his grandmother's name.

Monday night after work, I was getting into the shower when my phone ran; because of the many marketing people calling my phone, I didn't really think anything of it. With one leg already in the shower, I reached over to my cell phone, sitting on the vanity and pushed to accept the call. Upon accepting the call, I put it on speaker.

"Hello?" I said while trying to have my voice heard over the shower noise.

"Hello, this is (The rape victim's grandson) I got an email from you on Friday," he said with a concerned tone.

"Yes, yes!" As I jumped out of the tub and quickly turned the shower off.

"Yes, the son of the victim?"

"Well, that was my Grandmother."

"Sure, and you're the son of (Victim's name)?"

"Well, that was my father. He passed away."

"Sure. In 95' I believe."

"Who is this?" He says with concern wondering how I know so much about his family.

"My apology Sir. My name is Rashod Coleman, and I'm writing a book about an event from 1987, which involved your father and grandmother. Are you familiar with this event? I don't want to be the first one to tell you about it."

"I know vaguely about what you're talking about."

"Cool. I'll give you a quick run-down about what's going on. Daniel Coleman was arrested on February 21, 1987, for the raping and assaulting of your grandmother. He was also charged with kidnapping and assaulting a 22-year-old woman the same night around the corner from where your grandmother lived. Because both victims described the same black male's physical appearance and clothing, he was held for both crimes. After an investigation of DNA and fingerprints, it was determined that my Father did not commit the crime involving your grandmother. However, he was found guilty of committing the other crime and subsequently served 28-years in prison. After reviewing his files, I've found that he might have been falsely accused of this crime."

"OOOOOK," he said in a low tone.

"Well, I think the same person might have committed the crime. So, my question to you is, do you know if anyone was arrested for the heinous crime done to your grandmother?"

"I don't know."

"Well, is it possible for you to ask an uncle or someone that may know if there was ever anyone that was found guilty of committing that crime?"

A silence came out of the phone, and I couldn't interpret if it was a shocking silence or awkward silence. I interrupted the silence.

"Sir, if this puts you in a bad place, you don't have to do it."

"Yeah, I um, I just want to keep the PAST IN THE PAST."

"Thank you, sir, I won't hold you up any longer. I appreciate you reaching back out to me. I am still investigating it and writing the book, but I'll be sure to keep your families name out of it and from contacting you. Be blessed."

When he hung up the phone, I felt like Mike Tyson had given me his best shot to the stomach. This was my first interaction with anyone close to my father's case, and they were reluctant to provide me with any information. "Maybe he didn't know anything. Maybe it really put him in a bad place to think about his grandmother being brutally raped and beat as she screamed out for help."

As I sat on the side of the bed, I thought to myself, *as a police officer, I wanted to get to the bottom of every case I dealt with. When someone got away from me, I couldn't stop thinking about it. I still think about the robbery of the dollar tree and the young Puerto Rican family that had been robbed for their rent by a black male, 6ft, dark-skinned, black hoodie that pushed his way in the house while the mom was cooking and the kids were upstairs watching cartoons. As the gunman held the mom at gunpoint, she heard her kids coming downstairs, so she pointed the gunmen to rent money, which he took and fled on foot. Searching under every rock that night, we were unable to find him, and it bothers me to this day. But this guy had that mentality of a cop and was willing to let someone get away with raping his grandmother. Something just didn't seem right to me.*

I sent him a text before I went to sleep that said, "Thanks again for responding, and if any of your family or friends are willing to help me please, please give them my information."

He texted back, “Sure.”

CHAPTER 37

BRADY VS. MARYLAND

After hearing those words from the first person that had direct knowledge of the case, I felt defeated. I knew there had to be something out there for me to do. During a training at work, while I was daydreaming about the next steps I needed to take to free my father of this horrible label, our prosecutor made the statement, "When you make an arrest, be sure to tell us everything. No matter how big or small. We are handcuffed by the Brady vs. Maryland case law."

Brady vs. Maryland, I wondered to myself. I wonder what that is. During a short break in class, I went to speak to him.

"Excuse me, sir, you said Brady vs. Maryland, what is that exactly?"

"Brady vs. Maryland was a case law that says prosecutors need to hand over information that may show that the defendant is innocent. If we don't, we violate the right of the defendant, and that's illegal."

When we were released from the training, I quickly went to my vehicle and pushed the YouTube app to figure out what this case law was. I've been working in law enforcement for five years, and I have never heard of this before.

I researched the case, and a small summary of the case was as follows:

A guy named Brady and his Co-defendant Boblit murdered someone. Brady said Boblit did it, and Boblit said Brady did it. They were both going to be sent to prison because they were there, but when it came to sentencing purposes, the one who physically killed the man was going to get a harsher sentence. When the detectives interviewed Brady, he made four statements. All of his statements, he claimed that Boblit strangled the guy. Furthermore, when Boblit was interviewed, he made five statements. In four statements, he claimed that Brady strangled him and admitted that he had strangled the man in the 5th statement.

Before the trial, Brady's attorney approached the prosecutor to obtain the statements that his client's co-defendant Boblit had made to detectives. The prosecutor handed over four statements to Brady's lawyer and left the statement where Boblit admitted to being the killer out. Brady went to trial, lost, and was sentenced to life. Boblit then went to trial and lost also. After the trial, ironically, Brady's lawyer went back and looked at Boblit's trial transcript. Surprisingly he found the statement where Boblit admitted to the crime. Brady's lawyer went through his paperwork and saw that the prosecutor left that statement out of the discovery, which the prosecutor must hand over to the defense.

Brady's lawyer appealed the case under the grounds that the prosecutor purposely withheld information away from the defense that could have shown that the defendant was innocent. Similarly, to my father's case, the prosecutor objected to every argument that spoke of the suspect with the bloody coat and turn over the results of the DNA test which they, the prosecutors and police department, had within their possession before trial, according to FBI documents.

Within the Brady case, the supreme court said that withholding Boblit's statement was illegal and in violation of Brady's civil rights. They also ruled that prosecutors are not obligated to turn over every single piece of evidence. That's just not logical. They did, however, add certain elements that the evidence needs to have to be obligated to turn it over. They ruled that the evidence must be exculpatory (must exonerate the defendant), and in the state's hands at the time of the trial.

All of these elements were in my father's case as if his name was Brady, but because the system is designed unfairly, my father didn't get the benefit of the doubt as Brady did.

CHAPTER 38

AMERICAN MADE

The main question is, did my father commit these crimes? Did he brutally rape a 79-year-old woman as she slept in her bed? Did he beat and rape her, causing vaginal damage while breaking bones in her face from brutally punching her with a closed fist? Did he kidnap a young 22-year-old woman as she attempted to remove cash from an ATM at 4:30 in the morning? According to the very system I have sworn to uphold, they say he did.

But did he really do it? Why would someone else, matching the suspect's description, be running from the police carrying the very coat that was worn during a rape and a kidnapping. I will be the first to say that whoever committed these crimes shouldn't see the light of day, and that includes my father if it was him. But if a man is innocent, why would you lock him away? Why would you sentence him knowing that there are unanswered questions? And the most important question, why would you not think about his son Doodles? Was I that bad of a kid that I didn't deserve a father? Is my family cursed? Is my family not good enough to be complete like everyone else's family?

I know I am no exception when it comes to these kinds of situations. As of 2016, there were 2.3 million people incarcerated inside the United States. I am not saying that all those people were falsely accused of a crime they didn't commit, but even if there is one who is, that's too many. I understand the justice system's plan is to punish the person that does wrong, but what about his/her family? What about the sons and daughters that came into this world just wanting to have a good life?

My family has done well if I must say. We shed some tears, but we quickly found out that no one was coming to save us. We had to pull ourselves out of the dirt, lick our wounds, and move the family forward, even if that meant leaving my father behind. The system wanted to break us, but we refused to be broken. We refused to let anything or anyone, no matter how powerful they are, break us.

The End.

I tried for two years to get answers about the early morning of February 21, 1987. I've met with countless attorneys and innocent projects, but we have not received any answers. Once most people hear who the powerful prosecutor is, they are reluctant to even touch the case. My father is out of prison and hasn't even had speeding tickets since he's been released. He works every day, and he and my mother have reunited and remarried. But this doesn't mean we are stopping the fight to clear his name. A wise man once said, "What happens in the dark will come to light," and I pray for that day. I am no longer a Fatherless Son.

Since the conclusion of this book, I have continued my path in not only advocating for children of incarcerated parents but also advocating for legislation to change to make the appeals process easier. I am no longer with the Philadelphia Police Department. Still, my current Law Enforcement agency has allowed me to continue volunteering in middle and high schools, which is the joy of my life right now. My father is still on a monitoring system, but we are working diligently every day to one day clear his name. Also, be on the lookout for my next book, Teaching Your Black Child How to Survive Police Encounters. Stay updated by joining my mailing list at AuthorRashod@gmail.com or follow me on Facebook at Author Rashod Coleman Support Group for People with Incarcerated Parents.

Acknowledgments

First, I want to thank the woman that birthed me: Linda Ann Coleman, I know children can't choose, but if I could, I would prefer you to be my mother 100% of the time. I still can't understand how you're not mad at the world, but then again, that wouldn't be you. Some of the best advice you've ever given me was, "Take the positive traits from all the men in your life and use them to replace what you didn't from your father." I can't even measure how vital that advice was.

Secondly, I want to recognize and thank the following guys from third and Broom street: Jabbar, Wolly, Lover, Hock, D-nice, Fat Dave, Fat Kev, Smooth, L, Casime, Wayne and Pete. If it wasn't for all of you guys being loyal friends, and willing to go above and beyond to protect everyone on that street, who knows where I would be. At one point and time, we couldn't see ourselves living to the age of 21. Though most of us had no clue what it was like to have a loving father in the house, we are doing our best with the children we are raising. To T-Doc, Omar, Lenny, and L, I wish you guys were here to mature with us. But unfortunately, that's how things go in the inner-city go. You're lucky if you make it out. I love you, guys, and I wish you all the best.

Last but not least, I want to thank my wife and three children that support me in every endeavor that I take on. A lot of the reason I want to do any and everything is because I've always felt so locked and shackled down by Third Street. Now that I have figured out I can do whatever the hell I want, I want to do it all. Hopefully, I'm pulling my weight as a husband and a father. I have no clue what I'm doing, but it seems to be going well. I love all five of you guys, including the Dog.

References

Caught a body:
An individual that has killed someone

Stiff Jab:
Similar to a stiff arm in football.

Bloop ride:
Drug attics allowing some to use their vehicle in exchange for money

Resources:
Original Police Reports:

Always start by requesting the report from the arresting department. If the individual is locked up, they can still request their information and send it to you.

Court Documents:

You can contact the courthouse where they were tried and request all of the court documents from trial. It's one thing to listen to court testimony, but it's another thing to read it. Just because you paid a lawyer doesn't mean someone had the best representation.

Freedom Of Information Act-https://efoia.fbi.gov/#home

(When requesting something from the FBI, try to be specific as possible in regards to what you are asking for. I.e., in regards to First Name, Last Name, DOB, I am searching for the DNA results from the evidence of a crime submitted by ABC Police Department on 01/02/2003.)

Finding help-https://www.innocenceproject.org/

Note*

They usually give priority to individuals currently incarcerated. If the person you are researching has been released, he/she can gather the information themselves. If you don't have the money to retrieve them, don't be afraid to ask people that you don't know via Social Media.

Brady vs. Maryland- https://www.oyez.org/cases/1962/490 (Prosecutor withholding evidence)